The Essential

HOW

TO

KNOW GOD

THE ESSENTIAL DEEPAK CHOPRA SERIES

The Essential Ageless Body, Timeless Mind

The Essential How to Know God

The Essential Spontaneous Fulfillment of Desire

FUNDAMENTAL PRINCIPLES FROM THE
ORIGINAL BESTSELLING BOOK

DEEPAK CHOPRA

The Essential

HOW

TO

KNOW GOD

The Soul's Journey into the
Mystery of Mysteries

Harmony Books *New York*

Published in the United States by Harmony Books, an imprint of the
Crown Publishing Group, a division of Random House, Inc., New York.

www.crownpublishing.com

This is an abridged edition of *How to Know God:
The Soul's Journey into the Mystery of Mysteries,*
published in hardcover in the United States by Harmony Books,
an imprint of the Crown Publishing Group,
a division of Random House Inc., New York, in 2000.

HARMONY BOOKS is a registered trademark and the Harmony Books
colophon is a trademark of Random House, Inc.

Library of Congress Cataloging-in-Publication Data
is available upon request

ISBN 978-0-307-40774-0

Printed in the United States of America

Design by Lauren Dong

10 9 8 7 6 5 4 3 2 1

First Abridged Edition

For Herms Romijn

In what concerns divine things, belief is not appropriate.

Only certainty will do.

Anything less than certainty is unworthy of God.

—SIMONE WEIL

AUTHOR'S NOTE

THERE ARE FEW THINGS IN LIFE THAT I FIND more gratifying than learning and teaching. We are all born with an insatiable curiosity about the world around us, and I was fortunate to grow up in a home that encouraged that appetite. Now, as an adult, I enjoy the best of both worlds: I can explore science, ancient wisdom, health, and spirit on the one hand, and on the other I can share what I've learned—helping others to satisfy their own curiosities—through my books and lectures.

When I speak to audiences, I find myself presenting my ideas in a manner that is concise or expansive depending on the length of time I have at my disposal. A five-minute segment on a morning television show requires a very different presentation from an hour on my weekly Sirius radio program, which in turn is very brief compared to one of the week-long courses I teach around the globe. It occurs to me that the same holds true for what we read. After all, we don't always have the luxury of taking the time to explore the book-long articulation of a new idea, but we might have the time, say, to take in the essence of that idea.

It was from this thought that the Essential series was born. This series begins with three books that have attracted substantial followings in their expanded versions: *Ageless Body, Timeless Mind: The Quantum Alternative to Growing Old; How to Know God: The Soul's Journey into the Mystery of Mysteries; The Spontaneous Fulfillment of Desire: Harnessing the Infinite Power of Coincidence.* In these new essential volumes, I have distilled the most important elements from the full-length originals. It is my hope that this series will be of value to first-time readers of my work, as well as to those who may have already read these books, but wish to be inspired by these ideas all over again.

The Essential How to Know God: The Essence of the Soul's Journey into the Mystery of Mysteries explores the idea that God consciousness unfolds in seven stages. Each of these has value of its own, and each one bring us a step closer to full contact to the ultimate mystery, the mind of God. If God is a mirror in which we reveal ourselves to ourselves, which is my basic premise in these pages, then we see God as angry and judging when we ourselves are ruled by fear. In this same mirror we see God as endlessly loving when we arrive at an inspiring sense of our own limitless potential. In these pages I attempt to provide you, the reader, with a sense of this spiritual landscape, and ways to navigate it so you may experience your highest self. For this is the way to grant your self access to the ultimate reality, the state of infinite self-awareness where we come face to face with the Divine.

A REAL AND
USEFUL GOD

GOD HAS MANAGED THE AMAZING FEAT OF being worshiped and invisible at the same time. Although it doesn't seem possible to offer a single fact about the Almighty that would hold up in a court of law, somehow the vast majority of people believe in God—as many as 96 percent, according to some polls. This reveals a huge gap between belief and what we call everyday reality. We need to heal this gap.

What would the facts be like if we had them? They would be as follows. Everything that we experience as material reality is born in an invisible realm beyond space and time, a realm revealed by science to consist of energy and information. Something turns the chaos of quantum soup into stars, galaxies, rain forests, human beings, and our own thoughts. We will see that it is not only possible to know this source of existence but to become intimate and at one with it. When this happens, we will have the experience of God.

After centuries of knowing God through faith, we are now ready to understand divine intelligence directly. In many ways this new knowledge reinforces what spiritual traditions have already promised. God is invisible and yet performs all miracles. He is the source of every impulse of love. Beauty and truth are both children of this God. In the absence of knowing the infinite source of energy and creativity, life's miseries come into being. Getting close to God through a true knowing heals the fear of death, confirms the existence of the soul, and gives ultimate meaning to life.

Our whole notion of reality has actually been topsy-turvy. Instead of God being a vast, imaginary projection, he turns out to be the only thing that is real, and the whole universe, despite its immensity and solidity, is a projection of God's nature.

From the very beginning of religion in the West, it was obvious that God had some kind of presence, known in Hebrew as *Shekhinah*. Shekhinah formed the halos around angels and the luminous joy in the face of a saint. If God has a presence, that means he can be experienced. This is a huge point, because in every other way God is invisible and untouchable.

We personify God as a convenient way of making him more like ourselves. However, what could possibly give us confidence in any kind of benevolent spiritual Being when thousands of years of religion have been so stained by bloodshed?

We need a model that is both part of religion yet not bounded by it. Shaped like a reality sandwich, the following three-part scheme fits our commonsense view of God.

God

—————— TRANSITION ZONE ——————

Material world

Only the middle element of our scheme, called the transition zone, is new or unusual. A transition zone implies that God and humans meet on common ground. Somewhere miracles take place, along with holy visions, angels, enlightenment, and hearing the voice of God.

Materialist arguments against God remain powerful because they are based on facts, but they fall apart once you dive deeper than the material world. Dame

Julian of Norwich lived in England in the fourteenth century. Dame Julian asked God directly why he had created the world. The answer came back to her in ecstatic whispers:

> *You want to know your lord's meaning in what I have done? Know it well, love was his meaning. Who reveals it to you? Love. What did he reveal to you? Love. Why does he reveal it to you? For love.*

For Dame Julian, God was something to eat, drink, breathe, and see everywhere, as though she were an infatuated lover. Yet since the divine was her lover, she was elevated to cosmic heights, where the whole universe was "a little thing, the size of a hazelnut, lying in the palm of my hand."

When saints go almost mad with rapture, we find their expressions both baffling and yet very understandable. Although we have all gotten used to the absence of the sacred, we appreciate that journeys into the transition zone, the layer closer to God, continue to happen.

I don't believe saints and mystics are really so different from other human beings. If we look at our reality sandwich, the transition zone turns out to be subjective: This is where God's presence is felt or seen. Anything subjective must involve the brain, since it takes millions of neurons firing together before you can have any experience.

Now our search has narrowed down in a way that looks very promising: God's presence, his light, becomes real if we can translate it into a response of the brain, which I will call the "God response." Holy visions and revelations fall into seven definite events taking place inside the brain that give rise to beliefs. They bridge from our world to an invisible domain where matter dissolves and spirit emerges:

1. **Fight-or-flight response:** The response that enables us to survive in the face of danger. This response is linked to a God who wants to protect us. We turn to this God because we need to survive.

2. **Reactive response:** This is the brain's creation of a personal identity. From this response a new God emerges, one who has power and might, laws and rules. We turn to this God because we need to achieve, accomplish, and compete.

3. **Restful awareness response:** This is the brain's response when it wants peace. The divine equivalent is a God who brings peace. We turn to this God because we need to feel that the outer

world isn't going to swallow us up in its endless turmoil.

4. **Intuitive response:** We rely on our ability to know ourselves from the inside out. The God that matches this response is understanding and forgiving. We need him to validate that our inner world is good.

5. **Creative response:** The human brain can invent new things and discover new facts. We call this inspiration, and its mirror is a Creator who made the whole world from nothing. We turn to him out of our wonder at the beauty and formal complexity of Nature.

6. **Visionary response:** The brain can directly contact "the light," a form of pure awareness that feels joyful and blessed. The God that matches it is exalted. We need such a God to explain why magic can exist side by side with ordinary mundane reality.

7. **Sacred response:** The brain was born from a single fertilized cell that had no brain functions in it, only a speck of life. To match it, there is a God of pure being, one who doesn't think but just is. We need him because without a source, our existence has no foundation at all.

These seven responses, all very real and useful to us in our long journey as a species, form the unshakable basis of religion. No one can shoehorn God into a single box. We must have a range of vision as vast as human experience itself.

A subtle give-and-take is going on at the deepest level between parent and child. In the same way God seems to grow directly out of our deepest inner values. Peel away all the layers of an onion, and at the center you will find emptiness; peel away all the layers of a human being, and at the center you will find the seed of God.

I believe that God has to be known by looking in the mirror.

Although everyone's brain can create countless thoughts—just to take a number, at ten thoughts a minute, a single brain would conjure up more than 14,000 thoughts a day, 5 million a year, and 350 million in a lifetime. To preserve our sanity, the gross majority of these thoughts are repetitions of past thoughts, mere echoes. The brain is economical in how it produces a thought. Instead of having millions of ways, it has only a limited number. Physicists like to say that the universe is really just "quantum soup" bombarding our senses with billions of bits of data every minute. This swirling chaos must also be organized into a manageable number. So the brain, with its seven basic responses, provides more than sanity and meaning: it provides a whole world. Presiding over this self-created world is a God who embraces everything, but who also must fit into the brain's way of working.

In one way or another, when a person says the word *God,* he is pointing to a specific response from this list:

> *Any God who protects us like a father or mother stems from fight or flight.*
>
> *Any God who makes laws and rules over society stems from the reactive response.*
>
> *Any God who brings inner peace stems from the restful awareness response.*
>
> *Any God who encourages human beings to reach their full potential stems from the intuitive response.*
>
> *Any God who inspires us to explore and discover stems from the creative response.*
>
> *Any God who makes miracles stems from the visionary response.*
>
> *Any God who brings us back into unity with him stems from the sacred response.*

As far as I know, the brain cannot register a deity outside the seven responses. Why not? Because God is woven into reality, and the brain knows reality in these limited ways. It may sound as though we're reducing the Mystery of Mysteries to a firestorm of electrical activity in the cerebral cortex—but we aren't doing that. We are trying to find the basic facts that will make God possible, real, and useful.

Many people will be sympathetic to this because they long for a God who fits into their lives. No one can make God enter the everyday world, however. The real question is whether he might be here already and going unnoticed. I keep coming back to the transition zone in our "reality sandwich." Unless you are willing to take your vision there, the presence of God is too ghostly to be relied upon. Is the brain prepared for such a journey? Absolutely.

Can we truly satisfy the demands of objectivity when it comes to God? A physicist would recognize our reality sandwich with no difficulty. The material world has long since dissolved for the great quantum thinkers. After Einstein made time and space into fluid things that merge into each other, the traditional universe couldn't hold up. In the reality sandwich of physics there are also three levels:

Material reality, the world of objects and events

Quantum reality, a transition zone where energy turns into matter

Virtual reality, the place beyond time and space, the origin of the universe

It isn't just coincidence that these three layers parallel the religious worldview. The two models have to parallel each other, because they are both delineated by the brain. Science and religion are not really opposites but just very different ways of trying to decode the universe. Mystics journey into the transition zone closer to God, and while we might visit there for a few moments of joy, mystics have found the secret of remaining there far longer.

Existence breaks through its drab routine with a surge of bliss and purity. Some mystics describe these moments as timeless.

But what if we could steady our flash of ecstasy and learn to explore this strange new territory? In other words, the sacred isn't a feeling, it is a place. The problem is that when you try to journey there, material reality keeps pulling you back again.

Let me bring these abstract terms down to earth. Some of the following experiences have occurred to all of us:

In the midst of danger, you feel suddenly cared for and protected.

You deeply fear a crisis in your personal life, but when it comes, you experience a sudden calmness.

A stranger makes you feel a sudden rush of love.

An infant or young child looks into your eyes, and for a second you believe that an old soul is looking at you.

In the presence of death, you feel the passing of wings.

Looking at the sky, you have a sense of infinite space.

Whenever you have any such experiences, your brain has responded in an unusual way; it has responded to God.

If we only knew it, God's most cherished secrets are hidden inside the human skull—ecstasy, eternal love, grace, and mystery.

To find a window to God, you have to realize that your brain is layered into regions that are ruled by different impulses. The new kingdoms are full of higher thought, poetry, and love. The old kingdoms are more primordial, ruled by raw emotion, instinct, power, and survival.

In the old kingdoms each of us is a hunter.

The oldest hunter lurking in our brains is after bigger prey, God himself. And the motive isn't to fight or die but to find our speck of joy and truth that nothing in the world can erase. The one thing we cannot survive is chaos.

We evolved to find God.

Your brain is hardwired to find God. *Until you do, you will not know who you are.* There is a catch, however. Our brains don't lead us automatically to spirit.

It is typical of modern life to believe that nature is set up to be random and chaotic. This is far from true. Life looks meaningless when you have worn out old responses, old realities, and an old version of God. To bring God back, we have to follow new, even strange responses wherever they lead us. As one spiritual teacher wisely put it, "The material world is infinite, but it is a boring infinity. The really interesting infinity lies beyond."

God is another name for infinite intelligence. To achieve anything in life, a piece of this intelligence must be contacted and used. In other words, *God is always there for you.* The seven responses of the human brain are avenues to attain some aspect of God. Each level of fulfillment proves God's reality *at that level.*

Level 1 (Fight-or-Flight Response)
> You fulfill your life through family, community, a sense of belonging, and material comforts.

Level 2 (Reactive Response)
> You fulfill your life through success, power, influence, status, and other ego satisfactions.

Level 3 (Restful Awareness Response)
> You fulfill your life through peace, centeredness, self-acceptance, and inner silence.

Level 4 (Intuitive Response)
> You fulfill your life through insight, empathy, tolerance, and forgiveness.

Level 5 (Creative Response)
> You fulfill your life through inspiration, expanded creativity in art or science, and unlimited discovery.

Level 6 (Visionary Response)
> You fulfill your life through reverence, compassion, devoted service, and universal love.

Level 7 (Sacred Response)
> You fulfill your life through wholeness and unity with the divine.

It is very important to absorb this notion that spirit involves a constant process. It isn't a feeling, nor is it a thing you can hold and measure.

A striking example that there is a reachable place beyond material reality is prayer. Beginning more than twenty years ago, researchers devised experiments to try to verify whether prayer had any efficacy.

Researchers found that surgical patients' recovery could be from 50 to 100 percent better if someone prayed for them.

Of all the clues God left for us to find, the greatest is the light, the Shekhinah. From that clue we can unfold a true picture of the deity. This is a bold claim, but it is corroborated by the fact that science—our most credible modern religion—also traces creation back to light. In this century Einstein and the other pioneers of quantum physics broke through the barrier of material reality to a new world, and in their awe most had a mystical experience. They sensed that when light gave up its mysteries, God's light would be known.

Our vision can't help but be organized around light. The same brain responses that enable you to see a tree as a tree, instead of as a ghostly swarm of buzzing atoms, also enable you to experience God. They reach far beyond organized religion. But we can take any passage from world scripture and decode it through the brain. It is the mechanism that makes the scripture real to us. Our brains respond on the same seven levels that apply to our experience:

1. A level of danger, threat, and survival.
2. A level of striving, competition, and power.
3. A level of peace, calm, and reflection.
4. A level of insight, understanding, and forgiveness.
5. A level of aspiration, creativity, and discovery.
6. A level of reverence, compassion, and love.
7. A level of unbounded unity.

Every Bible story teaches something at one or more of these levels (as do all world scriptures), and in every instance the teaching is attributed to God. Your brain and the deity are thus fused in order for the world to make sense.

If you believe in a punishing, vengeful God—clearly related to fight or flight—you won't see the reality of the Buddha's teaching of Nirvana. If you believe in the God of love envisioned by Jesus—rooted in the visionary response—you will not see the reality of the Greek myth wherein Saturn, primal father of the gods, ate all his children. Every version of God is part mask, part reality. The infinite can only reveal a portion of itself at any one time.

The most startling conclusion of our new model is that God is as we are. The whole universe is as we are, because without the human mind, there would be only quantum soup, billions of random sensory impressions. Yet thanks to the mind/brain, we recognize that encoded into the swirling cosmos are the most valued things in existence: form, meaning, beauty, truth, love. These are the realities the brain is reaching for when it reaches for God. He is as real as they are, but just as elusive.

If asked why we should strive to know God, my answer would be selfish: I want to be a creator. This is the ultimate promise of spirituality, that you can become the author of your own existence, the maker of personal destiny. Your brain is already performing this service for you unconsciously. In the quantum domain your brain chooses the response that is appropriate at any given moment. The universe is an overwhelming chaos. It must be interpreted to make sense; it must be decoded.

To know God, you must consciously participate in making this journey—that is the purpose of free will. On the surface of life we make much more trivial choices but pretend that they carry enormous weight. In reality, you are constantly acting out seven fundamental choices about the kind of world you recognize:

The choice of fear if you want to struggle and barely survive.

The choice of power if you want to compete and achieve.

The choice of inner reflection if you want peace.

The choice to know yourself if you want insight.

The choice to create if you want to discover the workings of nature.

The choice to love if you want to heal others and yourself.

The choice to be if you want to appreciate the infinite scope of God's creation.

I am not arranging these from bad to good. You are capable of all these choices; they are hardwired into you. But for many people, some part of their brains is dormant, and therefore their view of spirit is extremely limited. It is no wonder that finding God is called *awakening*. A fully awakened brain is the secret to knowing God. In the end, however, the seventh stage is the goal, the one where pure being allows us to revel in the infinite creation of God. Here certainty can replace doubt, and as the inspired French writer Simone Weil once wrote about the spiritual quest, "Only certainty will do. Anything less than certainty is unworthy of God."

2

MYSTERY OF MYSTERIES

This is the work of the soul that most pleases God.
— THE CLOUD OF UNKNOWING

THE MYSTERY OF GOD WOULDN'T EXIST IF THE
world wasn't also a mystery. Some scientists believe
we are closer than ever to a "Theory of Everything," or
TOE, as the physicists dub it. TOE will explain the
beginning of the universe and the end of time. Is
there a place for God in this "everything," or does the
Creator get booted out of his own creation?

Anyone could be forgiven for thinking that God is
nowhere to be found here, that all the wonders of the
sacred world will become mundane.

For centuries the sacred was real, a source of

supreme power. Today what do we see instead? A society that strip-mines old myths to build a city like Las Vegas. If you want to meet myth here, you check into a hotel-casino called Excalibur.

In a mythless world, something is missing, but do we know what it is? No one can stand before the Great Pyramid of Cheops without feeling the presence of a power that is absent even in the hugest skyscraper.

From time immemorial humans have worried over the same questions: Do I have a soul? Is there an afterlife, and will I meet God when I get there? The Great Pyramid was an answer erected in stone. "Now tell me I'm not immortal!"

Fortunately, the most solid, reliable things in existence—a seashell, a pothole in the middle of the road—partake of God's mystery. If you believe in a rock, you are automatically believing in God.

Ordinary reality is only the top layer of our sandwich. The material world is full of familiar objects that we can see, feel, touch, taste, and smell. As big objects become very small, shrinking to the size of atoms, our senses fail us. Theoretically the shrinkage has to stop somewhere, because no atom is smaller than hydrogen, the first material particle to be born out of the Big Bang. But in fact an amazing transformation happens beyond the atom—everything solid disappears. Atoms are composed of vibrating energy packets that have no solidity at all, no mass or size. The Latin word for a packet or package is *quantum,* the word chosen to describe one unit of energy inside the atom, and, as it turned out, a new level of reality.

It is strange enough to hold up your hand and realize that it is actually, at a deeper level, invisible vibrations taking place in a void. Even at the atomic level all objects are revealed as 99.9999 percent empty space. On its own scale, the distance between a whirling electron and the nucleus it revolves around is wider than the distance between the earth and the sun. But you could never capture that electron anyway, since it too breaks down into energy vibrations that wink in and out of existence millions of times per second. Therefore the whole universe is a quantum mirage, winking in and out of existence millions of times per second. At the quantum level the whole cosmos is like a blinking light.

Quantum flashes are millions of times too rapid for us to register, so our brains play a trick on us by "seeing" solid objects that are continuous in time and space.

You and I exist as flashing photons with a black void in between each flash—the quantum light show comprises our whole body, our every thought and wish, and every event we take part in. Who is behind this never-ending creation? Whose power of mind or vision is capable of taking the universe away and putting it back again in a fraction of a second?

The power of creation—whatever it turns out to be—lies even beyond energy, a force with the ability to turn gaseous clouds of dust into stars and eventually into DNA. In the terminology of physics, we refer to this pre-quantum level as *virtual*. When you go beyond all energy, there is nothing, a void. Visible light becomes virtual light; real space becomes virtual space; real time becomes virtual time. In the process, all properties vanish. Light no longer shines, space covers no distance, time is eternal. This is the womb of creation, infinitely dynamic and alive. Words like *empty, dark,* and *cold* do not apply to it. The virtual domain is so inconceivable that only religious language seems to touch it at all.

Physics has struggled hard with this state that comes before time and space, and so has popular imagination. It may surprise many to learn that the familiar image of God as a patriarch in a white robe seated on his throne has little authority, even in Judaic scripture. The image appears only once, in the Book of Daniel, whereas we are told many times in the books of Moses that God is without human form.

The best working theory about creation reads as

follows: Before the Big Bang space was unbounded, expanded like an accordion into infinite pleats or dimensions, while time existed in seed form, an eternal presence without events and therefore needing no past, present, or future. This state was utterly void in one sense and utterly full in another. It contained nothing we could possibly perceive, yet the potential for everything resided here. As the Vedic seers declared, neither existence nor nonexistence could be found, since those terms apply only to things that have a beginning, middle, and end. Physicists often refer to this state as a *singularity:* space, time, and the entire material universe were once contained in a point.

Now if you can imagine that the cosmos exploded into being in a dazzling flash of light from this one point, you must then go a step further. *Because the pre-creation state has no time, it is still here.* The Big Bang has never happened in the virtual domain, and yet paradoxically all Big Bangs have happened—no matter how many times the universe expands across billions of light-years, only to collapse back onto itself and withdraw back into the void, nothing will change at the virtual level. This is as close as physics has come to the religious notion of a God who is omnipresent, omniscient, and omnipotent. *Omni* means all, and the virtual state, since it has no boundaries of any kind, is properly called the All.

In India seers often referred to it simply as That, or *tat* in Sanskrit. At the moment of enlightenment, a person is able to go past the five senses to perceive the only truth that can be uttered: "I am That, You are That, and all this is That." The meaning isn't a riddle; it simply states that behind the veil of creation, the pre-creation state still exists, enclosing everything.

A physicist friend once said to me: "You must realize, Deepak, that time is just a cosmic convenience that keeps everything from happening all at once. This convenience is needed at the material level, but not at deeper levels. Therefore if you could see yourself in your virtual state, all the chaos and swirling galaxies would make perfect sense. The whole cosmos has conspired to create you and me sitting here this very second."

Nothing is more fascinating than to watch science blurring its edges into spirit. Miracles indicate that reality doesn't begin and end at the material level.

In the Gospel of Thomas, Jesus says that his role in life is to point the disciples away from the rule of the five senses, which are totally confined to space-time:

I shall give you what no eye has seen and what no ear has heard and what no hand has touched and what has never occurred to the human mind.

In the blurring of the quantum and the miraculous, a single reality is beginning to emerge. A famous remark by Einstein puts it this way: "I want to know how God thinks, everything else is a detail." Because he was a rare visionary, I hope that Einstein would accept as a start the following map of how God thinks:

Virtual domain = the field of spirit

Quantum domain = the field of mind

Material reality = the field of physical existence

If you feel secure with these terms, you can clear up mystery after mystery.

The flow of reality is miraculous because invisible emptiness gets transformed into the brilliant orange of a butterfly's wing or the massive solidity of a mountain without any effort at all.

A real Theory of Everything would instruct us in the art of living on all three levels of reality with equal power and security. Saints strive to get to that point; it is the true meaning of enlightenment.

Faith in God is a way of opening the lines of communication beyond the material. So is prayer or hope. If there is ever going to be a science of miracles, it begins with intangibles that are rooted in spirit.

Once again I gaze upon the Great Pyramid of Cheops; only this time I see several ideas. The first is sheer spiritual audacity. Human beings aspire to be more than human.

The other idea behind the pyramid is wonder. Sacred sites tell us that we are wondrous creatures who should be doing wondrous works. And you can still see that here.

The Vertical Assembly Building at the Kennedy Space Center is tall enough to hold a Saturn V moon rocket upright and has proportions boggling the mind. This building is also an idea, the idea that we will find our origins and our cosmic family.

Giant rockets blast off. If a single bacterium comes back from deep space, we will have found our own cosmic seed. As the old myths wear out, new ones spring up in our souls. We crave to know that we are sacred once again. Are we? The deepest levels of the quantum domain are the common ground where our hands reach out to touch God. What we touch is divine, but it is also ourselves.

3

Seven Stages of God

If you don't make yourself equal to God,
you can't perceive God.

— ANONYMOUS CHRISTIAN HERETIC,
THIRD CENTURY

WE ARE NOW READY TO ANSWER THE SIMPLEST but most profound question: Who is God? One must assume that God leaves no fingerprints in the material world.

This gives us no choice but to find a substitute for infinity that retains something of God. The Book of Genesis declares that God created Adam in his own image, but we have been returning the favor almost since the beginning, fashioning God in our image over and over again. The same "I" that gives a person a sense of identity extending beyond the physical body, expanding to embrace nature, the universe, and ultimately pure spirit.

To anyone who worships God as the self, it is obvious that none of us are alone. The "self" isn't personal ego but a pervasive presence that cannot be escaped.

The God of any religion is only a fragment of God. There are seven versions of God, which can be associated with organized faiths.

Stage one: God the Protector

Stage two: God the Almighty

Stage three: God of Peace

Stage four: God the Redeemer

Stage five: God the Creator

Stage six: God of Miracles

Stage seven: God of Pure Being—"I Am"

Each stage meets a particular human need. In the face of nature's overwhelming forces, humans needed a God who would protect them from harm. When they felt that they had broken the law or committed wrongdoing, people turned to a God who would judge them and redeem their sins. In this way, purely from self-interest, the project of creating God in our own image proceeded—and continues to proceed.

We are not comparing religions here; no stage is absolute in its claim to truth. Each one implies a different relationship, however. In the progress from stage one to stage seven, the wide gap between God and his worshipers becomes narrower and eventually closes. Therefore we can say that we keep creating God in our image for a reason that is more than vanity; we want to bring him home to us, to achieve intimacy.

Unless we can see ourselves in the mirror, we will never see God there. Consider the list again, and you will see how God shifts in response to very human situations:

> *God is a protector to those who see themselves in danger.*
>
> *God is almighty to those who want power (or lack any way of getting power).*
>
> *God brings peace to those who have discovered their own inner world.*
>
> *God redeems those who are conscious of committing a sin.*
>
> *God is the creator when we wonder where the world came from.*

*God is behind miracles when the laws of nature
are suddenly revoked without warning.*

*God is existence itself—"I Am"—to those who
feel ecstasy and a sense of pure being.*

The issue isn't how many Gods exist, but how
completely our own needs can be spiritually fulfilled.
When someone asks, "Is there really a God?" the most
legitimate answer is, "Who's asking?" The perceiver
is intimately linked to his perceptions. From the
virtual level, which is our source, the qualities of
spirit flow until they reach us in the material world.
On the material plane, the brain is our only way of
registering reality, and spirit must be filtered through
biology.

Each of the seven kinds of response is a natural response of the human nervous system, and we were all
born with the ability to experience the entire range.

These are well-documented facts medically, but I
wish to take a step further. I contend that the brain
responds uniquely in every phase of spiritual life. Scientific research is incomplete at the higher stages of
inner growth, but we know that where the spirit leads,
the body follows. Faith healers do exist who transcend
medical explanation. Saints in every religion have been

observed to live on little or no food. Visions of God have been so credible that their wisdom moved and guided the lives of millions.

We can match each biological response, in fact, with a specific self-image:

RESPONSE	IDENTITY IS BASED ON ...
Fight-or-flight response	*Physical body/physical environment*
Reactive response	*Ego and personality*
Restful awareness response	*Silent witness*
Intuitive response	*The knower within*
Creative response	*Co-creator with God*
Visionary response	*Enlightenment*
Sacred response	*The source of all*

Looking at the right-hand column, you have a clear outline of the stages of human growth. It is undeniable that complete inner growth is a tremendous challenge. If you are trapped in traffic, blood boiling with frustration, higher thoughts are blocked out.

These higher responses we call more spiritual, but the brain is responding from the highest level it can. The deeper mystery centers on our ability to rise from an animal instinct to sainthood. Is this possible for everyone, or is the potential there only for the tiniest fraction of humanity? We will only find out by examining what each stage means and how a person rises up the ladder of inner growth.

Despite the enormous flexibility of the nervous system, we fall into habits and repeated patterns because of our reliance on old imprints. This is never more true than with our beliefs. In every religion there is the same streak of fear whenever a person is certain that the world is dominated by threat, danger, and sin. Yet every religion also contains the strain of love whenever the world is perceived as abundant, loving, and nourishing. It is all projection.

The wonder is that the human nervous system can operate on so many planes. We don't just navigate these dimensions, we explore them, meld them together, and create new worlds around ourselves. If you do not understand that you are multidimensional, then the whole notion of God runs off the rails.

Like a child growing up, we have to evolve toward a more complete vision, until the day arrives when we can see the whole as God does.

Reality itself may be only a symbol for the workings of God's mind, and in that case the "primitive" belief—found throughout the ancient and pagan world—that God exists in every blade of grass, every creature, and even the earth and sky, may contain the highest truth. Arriving at that truth is the purpose of spiritual life, and each stage of God takes us on a journey whose end point is total clarity, a sense of peace that nothing can disturb.

STAGE ONE:
GOD THE PROTECTOR
(Fight-or-Flight Response)

Neurologists have long divided the brain into old and new. The new brain is an organ to be proud of. When you have a reasoned thought, it is this area of gray matter, primarily the cerebral cortex, that comes into play. But the old brain wants its due; this is the part of us that claws for survival and is willing to kill, if need be, to protect us.

The old brain is reflected in a God who seems primordial and largely unforgiving. He knows who his enemies are; he doesn't come from the school of forgive and forget.

God is very dangerous in stage one; he uses nature to punish even his most favored children through storms, floods, earthquakes, and disease. Despite his frightening temper, God the protector was as necessary to life as a father is inside a family.

The old brain isn't logical. It fires off impulses that destroy logic in favor of strong emotions, instant reflexes, and a suspicious sense that danger is always around the corner. The favorite response of the old brain is to lash out in its own defense, which is why the fight-or-flight response serves as its main trigger.

In crisis we are all thrown back on a deep sense of physical danger. The loss of a job can feel like a matter of life and death. People wrangling over a bitter divorce at times act as if their former spouse has become a mortal enemy. The fact that the old brain exerts its influence age after age accounts for the durability of God's role as protector.

Because his role is to protect, the God of stage one fails when the weak fall prey to illness, tragedy, or violence. He succeeds whenever we escape danger and survive crisis. In the mood of triumph his devotees feel chosen. They exult over their enemies and once again feel safe (for a while) because heaven is on their side.

Reason teaches us that aggression begets retaliation—we know this undeniably, given the tragic history of war. But there is a wall between the logic of the new brain, which is based upon reflection,

observation, and the ability to see beyond bare survival, and the logic of the old brain. The old brain
fights first—or runs away—and asks questions later.

Who am I? . . .
A survivor.

At each stage the basic question, "Who is God?" im-
mediately raises other questions. The first of these is
"Who am I?" In stage one identity is based upon the
physical body and the environment. Survival is the
foremost consideration here.

When they asked, "Who am I?" the earliest writers
of scripture knew that they were mortals subject to
disease and famine. These conditions had to have a
reason; therefore the family relationship with God got
worked out in terms of sin, disobedience, and ignorance. Even so, God remained on the scene—he
watches over Adam and Eve, despite the curse put
upon them, and after a while he finds enough virtue in
their descendant Noah to save him from the sentence
of death.

Rather than viewing the God of stage one harshly,
we need to realize how realistic he is. Life has been incredibly hard for many people, and deep psychologi-

cal wounds are inflicted in family life. The God of
stage one salves these wounds and gives us a reason to
believe that we will survive. At the same time he fuels
our needs. As long as we need a protector, we will
cling to the role of children.

> *What is the nature of good and evil?* . . .
> Good is safety, comfort, food, shelter,
> and family.
> Evil is physical threat and abandonment.

An absolute standard of good and evil is something many people crave, particularly at a time when
values seem to be crumbling. In stage one, good and
evil seem to be very clear. Good derives from being
safe; evil derives from being in danger. But is the picture really so clear?

Social workers are well aware that abused children
have a strange desire to defend their parents. If you
try to remove the child from the abusive environment, he is deeply afraid that you are snatching away
his source of love. The old brain has an overriding
need for security, which is why so many abused wives
defend their husbands and return to them. Good and
evil become hopelessly confused.

The God of stage one is just as ambiguous.

Even if he is worshiped as a benign parent, one who never inflicted guilt upon us, his goodness is tainted by suffering. A father who provides with great love and generosity would be considered a good father, but not if he tortures one child. Anyone who considers himself a child of God has to consider this problem. Much of the time it is papered over.

How do I find God? . . .
Through fear and loving devotion.

If the God of stage one is double-edged, providing with one hand and punishing with the other, then he cannot be known only one way. Fear and love both come into play.

It takes a great deal of growing up before one can live with ambivalence and its constant blending of dark and light, love and hate—this is the road not taken in stage one.

Some children try to preserve innocence by denying that its opposite exists; they turn into idealists and wishful thinkers. They show a strong streak of denial when anything "negative" takes place and will remain anxious until the situation turns "positive" again.

Other children take sides, assigning all the anxiety-provoking traits to a bad parent while labeling the other as always good.

The good parent–bad parent solution takes the form of a cosmic battle between God and Satan. The division between the two makes for a much simpler story, as it does for a child who has decided that one parent must be the good one and the other bad.

The other coping strategy, which involves denying the negative and seeking always to be positive, is just as common in religion. A lot of harm has to be overlooked to make God totally benign, yet people manage to do so. The power of interpretation is linked to consciousness; things can't exist if you are not conscious of them. In religious terms the deity is still "perfect" (meaning that he is always right) because those he punishes must be wrong.

In stage one, God has to be right. If he isn't, the world becomes too dangerous to live in.

What's my life challenge? . . .
To survive, protect, and maintain.

Every stage of God implies a life challenge, which can be expressed in terms of highest aspiration. If you are surrounded by threats, to survive is a high aspiration. However, even in the worst situations a person aspires to do more than cope.

You might think that the next step would be escape. In stage one, however, escape is blocked by the reality principle. A child can't escape his family, just as famine victims often can't escape drought. So the mind turns instead to imitating God, and since God is a protector, we try to protect the most valuable things in life. In other words, stage one is the most social of all the seven worlds we will examine. Here one learns to be responsible and caring.

What is my greatest strength? . . .
Courage.

What is my biggest hurdle? . . .
Fear of loss, abandonment.

It isn't hard to figure out what you have to do to survive in a harsh world—you have to show courage in the face of adversity.

The devotee of a fearful God will not move on to a higher stage until he says, "I am tired of being afraid. You are not my God if I have to hide from your anger."

As organized religions demonstrate, it is possible to live a long time with an angry, jealous, unfair God, even though he is supposed to be the highest judge. Ultimately one must learn to live with ambivalence.

The important issue is psychological. How much fear are you willing to live with? When this hurdle is cleared, when personal integrity is more important than being accepted within the system, a new stage begins. Translate this to an inner war, with one voice urging rebellion and the other threatening you with punishment for breaking the law, and you have the core drama of stage one.

The central question in stage one: *Why did God have to make such a frightening world?* The answer doesn't lie with God but in our interpretation of him. To get out of stage one, you must arrive at a new interpretation of all the issues raised so far—Who is God? What kind of world did he create? Who am I? How do I fit in? In stage two the basic problem of survival has been overcome. There is much less need for fear, and for the first time we see the emerging influence of the new brain. Even so, just as the reptilian brain is buried inside the skull, not abolished by the cerebrum or canceled out by higher thought, the God of stage one is a permanent legacy that everyone confronts before inner growth can be achieved.

STAGE TWO:
GOD THE ALMIGHTY
(Reactive Response)

If stage one is about survival, stage two is about power. There is no doubt that God has all the power, which he jealously guards. At the beginning of the scientific era, when the secrets of electricity were being discovered and the elements charted, many worried that it was sacrilege to look too closely at how God worked. Power was not only his but rightfully so. Our place was to obey—a view that makes perfect sense if you consider heaven the goal of life. Who would endanger his soul just to know how lightning works?

Freud points out, however, that power is irresistible. The kind of God implied by the drive to power is dangerous, but he is more civilized than the God of stage one.

He is worshiped by those who have formed a stable society, one that needs laws and governance. The Almighty is not so willful as his predecessor; he still metes out punishment, but you can understand why—the wrongdoer disobeyed a law, something he knows in advance not to do. Justice is no longer so rough; the kings and judges who take their power from God do so with a sense of being righteous. They deserve their power—or so they tell themselves.

The drama of power is based on the reactive response, a biological need to fulfill ego demands. Studies in infant development demonstrate that babies do not simply learn to have a personal identity. Almost from the moment of birth some newborns are outgoing, demanding in their needs, bold, and curious about the outside world, while others are introverted, quiet, undemanding, and shy about exploring their environment. These traits persist and expand through childhood and in fact remain for life. This implies that the ego response is built into us.

The ruling dictum of the reactive response is "More for me." Taken too far, this leads to corruption, since eventually an insatiable appetite must run into the desires of others.

We find no altruistic gods in world mythology. The first commandment given to Moses is "You shall place no other God before me." Jehovah survives all competitors in the Old Testament. But in other systems, such as the Greek and the Hindu, the war for power is constant. The Judaic God is a surprising victor in his emergence from a small, conquered nation that had ten of its twelve tribes wiped off the face of the earth, yet the subjugated Hebrews projected a stable, unshakable God—the first God Almighty to survive all challengers.

Jehovah succeeded because he exemplified a world that was fast evolving—the world of competition and ambition. The God of stage two has structured a hierarchical world, one in which you can appeal to the king or the judge. The struggle to bring in laws to replace sheer might divides stage one and stage two, although there is always the threat of reversion. To prevent this we have a new God, an omnipotent judge who threatens even the most powerful king with retribution if he goes too far.

How do I fit in? . . .
I win.

The theme of stage two can be summarized as "Winning is next to godliness." The Almighty approves of accomplishment. The Protestant work ethic sealed his approval into dogma. Those who work the hardest will get the greatest reward. But did this belief actually derive from spiritual insight, or did people find themselves in a world where work needed to be done and added God's stamp of approval afterward?

If we take the Bible as our authority, there is

ample evidence to support the notion that God approves of work, competition, and winning. None of the kings of Israel is punished for going to war. In fact, most of the Old Testament victories require miracles or God's blessing to be achieved.

On the other hand, Jesus is adamantly opposed to war, and in general to work. The Sermon on the Mount is in favor of letting God handle all earthly needs.

> Do not store up for yourselves treasure on earth, where it grows rusty and moth-eaten, and thieves break in to steal it. Store up treasure in heaven instead. . . .

This sort of talk was disturbing. In the first place, it undercut the power of the rich.

Even if you ignore the letter of what is being said—society has found countless ways to serve God and money at the same time—Jesus doesn't equate power with achievement, work, planning, saving, or accumulation. All are necessary in order to build wealth, wage war, or divide the strong from the weak. These were the very goals Jesus did not want to further; therefore his rejection of power makes perfect sense. He wanted the human wolves to lie down with the lambs.

How do I find God? . . .
Awe and obedience.

Stage two is much less paralyzed by fear of God than stage one, but the next closest emotion to fear—awe—is much present. This new God punishes by the rules. Most of his rules make sense in broad outline; every society mandates against murder, theft, lying, and coveting property that belongs to someone else. As long as the deity inspires awe, the way to him is through blind obedience.

Every stage of God contains hidden questions and doubts. In this case the hidden question is: Can God really make good on his threats?

For fear of hurting ourselves, we pull away from disobedience, even though we have never experienced divine punishment in real life. To this end we take ordinary misfortunes such as illness, bankruptcy, and loss of loved ones, and interpret them as coming from God.

What is the nature of good and evil? . . .
Good is getting what you want.
Evil is any obstacle to getting what you want.

Obedience isn't an end unto itself. For obeying God's laws, the worshiper expects a reward. In stage two this takes the form of getting what you want. God permits you to fulfill your desires, and he makes you feel righteous in the bargain. In his role as Almighty, the deity now begins to answer prayers. In this value system, the rich can clothe themselves in virtue while the poor are morally suspect and seem shameful.

Measuring good and evil according to rewards has its pitfalls. The ego has to figure out how to aggrandize "me" while at the same time being good. Rarely does the solution emerge as pure honesty and cooperation.

As a result, manipulation is born. The goal of manipulation is to get what you want but not look bad in the process. This calculus is very important if you fear that God is watching and keeping tabs.

Are these simply the kinds of shortcuts we are all tempted to use in order to get our way? If you turn to the Old Testament, there is no mistaking that God himself is manipulative—praising those who hew to the law, withdrawing to show anger, sending an endless string of prophets to attack sin through preaching that stirs up guilt. We continue to use the same tactics in society, pressuring conformity to what the majority believe is good while disguising the evils that are done to the band of wrong-thinkers (pacifists, radicals, communists, etc.) who refuse to fall into line.

What is my life challenge? . . .
Maximum achievement.

Stage two isn't just a matter of naked power. It brings a sense of optimism to life. The world exists to be explored and conquered.

In stage two the ego is so bent on accomplishment that it ignores the threat of emptiness. Power for its own sake has no meaning, and the challenge of acquiring more and more power (along with its symbols in terms of money and status) still leaves a huge vacuum of meaning. This is why absolute loyalty is demanded by God at this stage—to keep the faithful from looking too deeply inside. The harder road would be to heal the disorder of our inner life. This is the choice that carries everyone from stage two to stage three.

What is my greatest strength? . . .
Accomplishment.

What is my biggest hurdle? . . .
Guilt, victimization.

Anyone who finds satisfaction in being an accomplished, skilled worker will find stage two a very tempting place to rest on the spiritual journey. Often the only ones who break free to a higher stage have had some drastic failure in their lives. Failure carries its own dangers, primarily that you will see yourself as a victim, which make the chances for spiritual progress worse than ever. But failure does raise questions about some basic beliefs in stage two. If you worked hard, why didn't God reward you? Does he lack the power to bestow good fortune—or has he forgotten you entirely? As long as such doubts don't arise, the God of stage two is the perfect deity for a competitive market economy. However, there is still the problem of guilt.

Despite its external rewards, stage two is associated with the birth of guilt. Someone has to lay down the commandments defining absolute right and wrong. Afterward, the law-abiding will enforce their own obedience.

Stage two brings the comfort of laws clearly set down, but it traps you into putting too much value on rules and boundaries, to the detriment of inner growth.

What is my greatest temptation? . . .
Addiction.

It's no coincidence that a wealthy and privileged society is so prone to rampant addictions. Stage two is based on pleasure, and when pleasure becomes obsessive, the result is addiction.

The God of stage two is jealous of his power over us because it pleases him. He is addicted to control. And like human addiction, the implication is that God is not satisfied, no matter how much control he exerts.

Psychiatrists meet people every day who complain about the emotional turmoil in their lives and yet are blindly addicted to drama. Other addictions are also based on behavior: the need to have something wrong in your life (or to create it if it doesn't exist), the obsession over things going wrong—this is the "what if" addiction—and finally the compulsion to be perfect at all costs.

This last addiction has taken secular form in people who crave the perfect family, perfect home, and perfect career. They do not even see the irony that such "perfection" can be bought only at the price of killing our inborn spontaneity, which by its nature can never be controlled.

When a person begins to see that life is more than trying to be perfect, the bad old desires rear their heads again. Only this time they are seen as natural, not evil, and the road is open for stage three. It comes as a source of wonder when turning inward breaks the spell of I, me, mine and ends its cravings.

STAGE THREE:
GOD OF PEACE
(Restful Awareness Response)

Whether unleashing floods or inciting warfare, the God we've seen so far relishes struggle. Obedience to him has mattered far more than our own needs.

The balance begins to shift when we find that we can meet our own needs. It takes no God "up there" to bring peace and wisdom, because the cerebral cortex already contains a mechanism for both. When a person stops focusing on outer activity, closes his eyes, and relaxes, brain activity alters. The dominance of alpha-wave rhythms signals a state of rest that is aware at the same time. Blood pressure and heart rate decrease, accompanied by lessened oxygen consumption.

These various changes do not sound overly impressive when put in technical terms, but the subjective effect can be dramatic. Peace replaces the mind's chaotic activity; inner turmoil ceases. Psalms declare, "Be still and know that I am God."

Only by discovering that peace lies within does

the devotee find a place that divine vengeance and retribution cannot touch. This forms the basis of contemplation and meditation in every tradition.

Who am I? . . .
A silent witness.

The God of stage three is a God of peace because he shows the way out of struggle. There is no peace in the outer world, which is ruled by struggle. People who attempt to control their environment—I am thinking of perfectionists and others caught up in obsessive behavior—have refused the invitation to find an inner solution.

One friend told me he had torn his Achilles tendon. But instead of being in excruciating pain, he felt extremely calm and detached.

It is common for people to break into stage three with this kind of abruptness. In place of an active, excited mind, they find a silent witness.

In between the pain and the brain something must intervene that decides how much discomfort is going to be felt. It is just as normal to feel no pain as to feel a great deal. To someone who has entered stage three, the decision maker is not a mystery. He is the presence of God bringing peace, and the pain being relieved is more than physical; it includes the pain of the soul caught in turmoil. By going inward, the devotee has found a way to stop that pain.

How do I fit in? . . .
I remain centered in myself.

In many ways finding your center is the great gift of stage three, and the God of peace exists to assure his worshiper that there is a place of refuge from fear and confusion.

A warrior God didn't solve the problem, nor did laying down countless laws. The God of peace can't simply dictate an end to strife and struggle. Either human nature has to change or else it must disclose a new aspect that transcends violence. In stage three the new aspect is centeredness. If you find your own inner quiet, the issue of violence is solved, at least for you personally. A friend of mine who has been deeply influenced by Buddhism goes even further: he says that if you can find the motionless point at your core, you are at the center of the whole universe.

My choices will dissolve in the wind once I give up this body. To realize this truth is to be free, so

Buddhism teaches. You are one step closer to finding out who you really are.

How do I find God? . . .
Meditation, silent contemplation.

The Old Testament clearly states that the way to peace is through reliance on God as an outside power. Giving up trust in God and looking instead to yourself could be very dangerous. It could also be heresy.

A few clues indicate that I can risk a different approach, however. In the Bible one finds such verses as "Seek ye the kingdom of heaven within." And the means of going inward, chiefly meditation and silent contemplation, are not that far removed from prayer.

There is no doubt that people resist the whole notion of God being an inner phenomenon. The vast majority of the world's faithful are firmly committed to stages one and two, believing in a God "up there," or at any rate outside ourselves. And the problem is complicated by the fact that going inward isn't a revelation; it is just a beginning. The quiet mind offers no sudden flashes of divine insight. Yet its importance is stated eloquently in the medieval document known as "The Cloud of Unknowing," written anonymously in the fourteenth century. The author tells us that God, the angels, and all the saints take greatest delight when a person begins to do inner work. However, none of this is apparent at first:

> *For when you first begin, you find just a darkness and, as it were, a cloud of unknowing. . . . This darkness and this cloud, no matter what you do, stands between you and your God.*

The only solution, the writer informs us, is perseverance.

We are advised to go into a "cloud of forgetting" about anything other than the silence of the inner world.

For centuries this document has seemed utterly mystical, but it makes perfect sense once we realize that the restful awareness response, which contains no thoughts, is being advocated.

The value of stage three lies more in promise than in fulfillment, because it is a lonely road. The promise is given by our anonymous writer, who emphasizes over and over that delight and love will eventually arise out of silence. The inner work is done for only one purpose—to feel the love of God—and there is no other way to achieve it.

What is my life challenge? . . .
To be engaged and detached at the same time.

Jesus wanted his disciples to be "in the world but not of it." He wanted them to be both detached and engaged—detached in the sense that no one could grab their souls, engaged in the sense that they remained motivated to lead a worthy life. This is the balancing act of stage three, and many people find it hard to manage.

The writer of "The Cloud of Unknowing" says that going within is not the real dilemma, nor is rejection of society and its values. Here is how our writer describes spiritual work:

> *Who is it that calls it nothing? Surely it is our outer man and not our inner. Our inner man calls it All; for it teaches him to understand all things bodily or spiritual, without any special knowledge of one thing in itself.*

This is a remarkable description of how silence works. We aren't talking about the silence of an empty mind—in fact, those who achieve inner silence are also thinking in the ordinary way. But the thought takes place against a background of nonthought. The mind is full of a kind of knowing that could speak to us about everything, yet it has no words; therefore we seek this knowingness in the background. If you keep to your plan, rejecting outward answers over and over, never giving up on your belief that the hidden goal is real, eventually your seeking bears fruit.

During this whole time, your work inside is private, but outer existence has to go on. Thus the balancing act Jesus referred to as being in the world but not of it. Or as we are stating it, being detached and engaged at the same time.

What is my greatest strength? . . .
Autonomy.

What is my biggest hurdle? . . .
Fatalism.

In stage three a person finds that he is autonomous. By breaking free of social pressures, he can be himself. Yet there is the risk of fatalism, a feeling that being free is just a form of isolation with no hope of influencing others. How can another person, someone not at this stage, understand what it means?

Gandhi, because he had renounced the outer trappings, couldn't be grabbed anywhere in the usual places. Those in power couldn't threaten him with losing his job, house, family, or even with imprisonment and death (they tried all of these means anyway). Detachment renders the use of power impotent. You validate yourself from within, and this equates with God's blessing. At this stage of inner growth, the power of going inward is veiled; there is darkness and a cloud of unknowing. Yet somehow the pull toward spirit is real. For all the outer sacrifices, something seems to have been gained. What that something is becomes clear later; at this moment there is a period of adjustment as the person accommodates to a new world so different from that of every day.

What is my greatest temptation? . . .
Introversion.

I've taken great pains to show that stage three is not about becoming an introvert. That is the great temptation, especially for those who misinterpret the words *going inward* and *inner silence.* Someone who by nature wants to shrink from the world can use as his excuse that spirituality should be inward. Someone who feels pessimistic in general can find comfort in rejecting the whole material world.

True renunciation is quite different. It consists of

realizing that there is reality behind the mask of the material world. The richest man in the world could be a renunciate, if he has the proper insights, while a greedy, selfish monk could fall very short of renuncia tion. The whole issue in stage three has to do with allegiance. Do you give your allegiance finally to the inner world or the outer? Many challenges come our way on this long journey, and no matter what answer you give verbally, it will be in the fire of experience that real answers come.

STAGE FOUR:
GOD THE REDEEMER
(Intuitive Response)

The higher stages of spirituality seem mysterious when framed this way, because there is nowhere to go beyond silence. We have to look at what silence can grow into, which is wisdom.

Psychologists are well aware that wisdom is a real phenomenon. If you pose a battery of problems to subjects who span a range of ages, the older ones will predictably give wiser answers than the younger. It doesn't matter really what the problem is. Wisdom is a perspective applied to any situation.

Just as stage three sees the birth of a peaceful God, stage four sees the birth of a wise God. In the role of God the Redeemer, he begins to take back all the judgments that weighed down life; therefore his wisdom creates a sense of being loved and nurtured. In this way the loneliness of the inner world begins to soften.

To a psychologist, wisdom is correlated with age and experience, but something much deeper is involved. Spiritual masters speak of "second attention." First attention is concerned with the task at hand. Second attention looks beyond the task at hand, somehow viewing life from a deeper perspective. From this source wisdom is derived, and the God of stage four appears only when second attention has been cultivated.

First attention organizes the surface of life; second attention organizes the deeper levels. The God of stage four enters one's life only after you make friends with the subconscious.

The big question is how we can learn to trust second attention. Once you start identifying with the knower—that part of yourself that is intuitive, wise, and perfectly at home in the quantum world—then God assumes a new shape. He turns from all-powerful to all-knowing.

Who am I? . . .
The knower within.

You will never trust your intuition until you iden tify with it.

A person who has arrived at stage four long ago gave up group values. The enticements of war, competition, the stock market, fame, and wealth have faded.

In stage four the emptiness of outward life is rendered irrelevant because a new voyage has commenced. The wise are not sitting around contemplating how wise they are; they are flying through space and time, guided on a soul journey that nothing can impede. The hunger to be alone, characteristic of anyone in stage four, comes from sheer suspense. The person cannot wait to find out what comes next in the unfolding of the soul's drama.

The word *redemption* conveys only a pale sense of how all-involving this whole expedition is. There is much more to the knower within than just being free from sin. Someone who still felt burdened with guilt and shame, however, would never embark on the voyage. You don't have to be perfect to try to reach the angels, but you do have to be able to live with yourself and keep your own company for long stretches of time. A sense of sin hinders that ability.

How do I fit in? . . .
I understand.

In stage three the inner world evidences little activity. Ships don't sail in a dead calm. They rest and wait. The inner world comes alive in stage four, where calmness and peace turn into something much more useful. One begins to understand how reality works, and human nature starts to unfold its secrets.

After paying enough attention (always the key word) you begin to see that events form patterns; you see that they also hold lessons or messages or signs and then you see that these outer events are actually symbols for inner events.

The conclusion of this little package of insight is that there are no victims. Wise people often say this, but when they declare that all is wisely and justly ordered, their listeners remain baffled. What about wars, fires, random murders, aircraft disasters, despotism, gangsters, and on and on?

Here is a good place to ask what the inner knower actually knows. As we commonly define it, knowledge is experience that has been recorded in memory.

Wisdom consists of being comfortable with certainty and uncertainty. In stage four life is spontaneous, yet it has a plan; events come as a surprise, yet they have an inexorable logic. Strangely, wisdom often arrives only after thinking is over. Instead of turning a situation over from every angle, one arrives at a point where simplicity dawns. In the presence of a wise person one can feel an interior calm, alive and breathing its own atmosphere. The New Testament calls this "the peace that passes understanding," because it goes beyond thinking —no amount of mental churning will get you there.

How do I find God? . . .
Self-acceptance.

The inner world has its storms, but much more terrible are its doubts. No one can get very far in stage four if there is self-doubt, because the self is all there is to rely on. Outside support has lost its reassurance. In ordinary life, such a loss is dreaded.

In stage four, however, all moorings are loosed.

Since infancy we have all gained security from having one mother, one father, our own friends, one spouse, a family of our own; this sense of attachment reflects a lifelong need for support.

In stage four the whole support structure melts away—the person is left to get support internally, from the self. Self-acceptance becomes the way to

God. If that involves giving up the old support systems, the person willingly pays the price. The soul journey is guided by an inner passion that demands its own fulfillment.

What is the nature of good and evil? . . .
Good is clarity, seeing the truth.
Evil is blindness, denying the truth.

From the outside someone in stage four seems to have opted out. With no social bonds left, there is really no social role, either. The deepest insights are usually not socially acceptable; therefore they are seen as insane, heretical, or criminal.

In stage four good is clarity of mind, which brings the ability to see the truth. Evil is blindness or ignorance, which makes the truth impossible to see.

The truth becomes a quest from which no one can deter you. Goodness means remaining true to your quest, evil is being drawn away from it. In the case of Socrates, even a sentence of death left him impervious. When offered an escape he refused. His evil would have been to betray himself. By drinking his cup of hemlock, Socrates died a traitor to the state who had upheld a total commitment to himself: this was a gesture of ultimate goodness.

What is my life challenge? . . .
To go beyond duality.

I have saved the topic of sin until we understood the inner world better. Sin is a stubborn issue. Because no one was perfect in childhood, we all carry the imprints of guilt and shame.

Sin can be defined as a wrong that leaves an impression. In the East any act that leaves an impression is called karma; this is a much broader definition than sin and it includes no moral blame. Karma can be right or wrong and still leave an imprint.

The God of stage four, intent on redemption, sees sinners and saints in the same light, and all actions as equal. This valuation is scandalous. Society exists to draw the line between right and wrong, not to erase it. When Jesus pared the hundreds of Jewish laws down to two (put no other gods before God and love your neighbor as yourself), the good people around him assumed he was either crazy or criminal.

In actuality, he was extremely responsible. In one phrase—"As you sow, so shall you reap"—Jesus stated the law of karma quite succinctly. He had no intention of getting away with wrongdoing but instead pointed to a higher spiritual rule: your actions today define your future tomorrow. This dynamic turns out to be more important than identifying sin.

What, then, would forgiveness of sin amount to? Finding the answer is the life challenge of this stage. A redeemed soul sees itself as new and unblemished. To reach this state of innocence would be impossible according to the law of karma, for the cycle of sowing and reaping never ends.

In theory at least the answer is simple: you redeem your soul by turning to God. God transcends karma because he alone isn't in the cosmos.

One doesn't need to repeal the law of karma at all. The instant they wake up in the morning, a saint and a sinner are in the same place. This place stands outside reward and punishment. In stage four your challenge is to find this place, hold on to it, and live there. When you have accomplished this task, duality is gone. In Christian terms, your soul is redeemed and returned to innocence.

What is my greatest strength? . . .
Insight.

What is my biggest hurdle? . . .
Delusion.

The inner quest is all about undoing attachments. These do not come free all at once, nor is every attachment equal. It is entirely normal to arrive at profound insights about yourself and still feel as ashamed or guilty as a little child over certain things.

Stage four requires new tactics. No one outside yourself can offer absolution. To get past an obstacle requires your own insight. There is only one insight and one delusion in stage four. The insight is that everything is all right; the delusion is that we have made unforgivable mistakes. In the eyes of God, all souls are innocent. The same reason tells us that we are deluded to keep holding on to past mistakes. They cannot blemish our souls, and their residual effect, in terms of guilt, shame, and payback, will be washed away in good time.

What is my greatest temptation? . . .
Deception.

Every stage of inner growth contains more freedom than the one before. Breaking free from sin is a great accomplishment in stage four, but the price of redemption is constant vigilance.

It takes more than an act of will to escape notions

of right and wrong. The process has to continue without deception. There is a lot of work to do in the form of meditation, self-reflection, taking responsibility. Every step forward must be tested, and the temptation to go backward persists until the very end.

The whole process of being true to yourself brings as its reward a higher level of awareness. At this level, the issues of duality have been left behind, and when that happens, the subjective feeling is one of being redeemed.

STAGE FIVE:
GOD THE CREATOR
(Creative Response)

There is a level of creativity that goes far beyond anything we have discussed so far. It dawns when intuition becomes so powerful it must break out into the environment. This "super-intuition" controls events and makes wishes come true, as though an artist is working not in paint and canvas but in the raw material of life.

Now the time has come when fate no longer has to be hidden from view. This happens when a person gives up all notions of accident, coincidence, and random events, and instead claims responsibility for each and every incident, however trivial. Events no longer happen "out there" but are guided by one's own intentions. Stage five joins the individual to God in a partnership as co-creators.

This is the most intimate God we have projected so far, because of a quality that is the key to stage five: openness. God the Creator is willing to share his power with his creation. Our minds have to grasp just what it means to have all of time and space at our disposal.

To be in alliance with God, you must uphold your side of the partnership, which involves some very specific beliefs:

You have to see yourself at the center of the creative process.

You have to accept responsibility for all outcomes.

You have to identify with a larger self than the one living here and now in this limited physical body.

Many people on the spiritual path willingly accept one or more of these beliefs, but the deciding factor is whether you live them out. This is a stage of power, and that implies getting straight about whether you deserve to wield it.

It is surmised that when people are in a creative state, the cerebral cortex first establishes restful awareness. Unlike other periods of relaxation, this state is on the lookout for something—a stroke of inspiration—and when it occurs a spike of activity is registered by the mind. Truly creative people tend to introduce a question into their minds and then wait for the solution to arrive—hence the necessity of going into a relaxed mode.

By stage five, a person realizes that God is not a being with desires. The inhibitions that hold us back—and this holds true at every level of growth— exist inside ourselves. God sees all choices with the same eye—his vision includes no judgment. When a person realizes this, God suddenly opens his deepest secrets, not because God changed his mind but because our perspective has.

How do I fit in? . . .
I intend.

If we get down to specifics, the act of creation is reducible to one ingredient: intention. There are no magic tricks to making a thought come true, no secrets of miracle-working. You just intend a thing and it happens. When highly successful people are interviewed, many times they repeat the same formula: "I had a dream and I stuck with it, because I was certain that it would come true." Of course, there is a great deal of work to be done to arrive at any great accomplishment, but in stage five the end result is preordained, and therefore the work itself isn't primary. It's just what you need to do to get to the goal. Whatever it feels like, intention lies at the heart of the process.

Making any idea come to life always involves intention. If you have a flash of genius, that flash remains inside your head until it materializes. So the important issue is how it gets materialized. There are efficient ways and inefficient ways. The most efficient way is shown to us by the mind itself. If I ask you to think of an elephant, the image just appears in your head, and even though millions of neurons had to coordinate this image, using chemical and electromagnetic energy, you remain aloof from that. As far as you are concerned, the intention and the outcome are one; all intervening steps remain invisible.

Now consider a larger intention, such as the intention to go to medical school. Between having this idea initially and fulfilling it are many steps, and these are not internal at all: raising tuition money, passing exams, gaining admission, etc. Yet, just like the image of the elephant, each of these steps depends upon brain operations being invisibly coordinated. You think, move, and act using intention. In stage five this automatic pilot is extended to the outer world. That is, you expect the entire process of becoming a doctor to unfold with the least effort, unhindered by obstacles. The boundary between "in here" and "out there" is softened. All events take place in the mind field first and then exhibit their outward manifestation.

Your role is to remain as sensitive and alert as possible. The turning points in life arrive as small signals at first. So being vigilant about tiny clues is a major part of spiritual evolution. God always speaks in silence, but sometimes the silence is louder than at other times.

How do I find God? . . .
Inspiration.

I often hear people quote Joseph Campbell's advice to "follow your bliss." In stage five bliss becomes better defined as inspiration. Rather than having intentions that originate with your ego, you feel that you are called to do something highly meaningful. The sense of being outside yourself is often present and, as God takes over, the fruition of your desires feels blissful—whereas the fulfillment of ego desires often surprises us by feeling very flat: ask anyone how they feel six months after winning the lottery.

To be inspired is a high state of attainment. Four decades ago, the psychologist Abraham Maslow first spoke of *peak experiences,* his terminology for a breakthrough into expanded consciousness. A peak experience shares many qualities with inspiration, including feelings of bliss and being outside oneself. The conscious mind receives a supercharged burst from the unconscious, and even though this may happen only once in a lifetime, that feeling of empowerment can influence the course of events for many years.

Although Maslow theorized that peak experiences gave glimpses of the real norms of the psyche, it was nearly impossible to prove that anyone lived at a peak for any length of time. Out of the whole population, Maslow and like-minded researchers could barely find 5 percent who even temporarily made such a transition. Such individuals felt as a normal experience that they were safe, confident, full of esteem for themselves and others, deeply appreciative of what life brought to them, and constantly in a state of wonder that the world could remain so fresh and alive every day, year in and year out.

To redefine human nature in such positive terms seemed unrealistic. Freud had already laid down as law that human nature contains hidden tendencies that break out like caged monsters.

Maslow himself, believing with all his heart that human nature is trustworthy and capable of great inner growth, had to admit that tremendous obstacles stand in our way. Most people are too needy to grow, because as long as our needs are frustrated, we spend most of our time being driven to fulfill them. Need comes in four levels, Maslow said: the first is physical, the need to feed and clothe ourselves; next comes the need for safety, followed by the need to be loved, and finally by the need for self-esteem. Only at the top of the pyramid does a person get the chance to feel self-actualized.

When someone turns to God in order to feel safe or to be loved, need is the real motivation. In any event, God doesn't intervene to rectify the situation. To be driven by need is just how life works. To bring back the sacred, it must accomplish something that love, security, self-esteem, or good fortune cannot. When we are inspired, we don't act from need at all.

You don't have to be spiritually advanced to feel

triumphant when you reach the top of Everest or win the Nobel Prize. Spiritual advancement shows up when the small things carry a share of blessing, too.

What is my life challenge? . . .
To align with the Creator.

If we assume that our quantum model holds good, then nothing is unholy. Beyond right and wrong, the Creator may permit us to explore anything he himself has allowed to exist.

In stage five, although one may be able to make almost any wish come true, the ones that *should* come true matter more. Here we are guided to increase bliss, love, charity to others, and peaceful existence on the planet. An inner sense of rightness must be cultivated; an inner sense of ego must be diminished. The larger will that rules events always tries to make itself known. If you align with it, the path through this phase is smooth; if you don't, there are many ups and downs, and your ability to manifest your desires can run into as many obstacles as it overcomes.

What is my greatest strength? . . .
Imagination.

What is my biggest hurdle? . . .
Self-importance.

Artists who create with paint or music start with a blank canvas or page; they go inward and an image appears, at first faint but growing. The image carries a feeling with it of wanting to be born. If the inspiration is genuine, this impression never fades. Creator, creation, and the process of creating are fused.

In stage five the fusing isn't complete. There is the danger of trying to take over the process, which severs the alliance with God.

Struggles with self-importance can last a long time, but they always end once the person finds a way to give more of the responsibility back to God. In other words, the way to power is to give up power. This is the great lesson the ego is confronted with in this phase.

STAGE SIX:
GOD OF MIRACLES
(*Visionary Response*)

I once read in an inspirational book the following: *This is a recreational universe. Your ability to play in it is limited only by how much you can appreciate.* On reading these words it occurred to me that the world's greatest saints and masters may be simply enjoying themselves.

Yet for all their miracles, or because of them, we think of saints as being without fun, loving relationships, sexual impulses. It's impossible to imagine a saint with money and a good car.

In stage six all of these assumptions are tested. Full-blown miracles are now possible. For example, a nun of the late Victorian era named Sister Marie of Jesus Crucified had the alarming habit of suddenly swooping up to the tops of trees, where she flitted from branch to branch like a bird. This feat embarrassed Mariam, since she had no way of predicting or controlling her ecstasies, and on at least one occasion (eight were observed in total), Mariam timidly asked her companion to turn her back and not look.

In stage six, a person returns to the word, in all its primordial power, to discover the source. Behind everything is a vibration—not in the sense of a sound or an energy wave, because those are material, but a "mother vibration" at the virtual level that includes everything. In India the sound of the divine mother took the name *om,* and it is believed that meditating on this sound will unlock all the mother's secrets.

What brain mechanism, if any, gives visions of God and makes miracles possible? Some researchers have speculated that the two hemispheres of the brain become completely balanced in higher states of consciousness.

So what we are left with is an elusive brain function that I will call the visionary response. It is marked by the ability to change energy states outside the body, causing objects and events to be transformed. No brain researcher has come within miles of describing the necessary shift that must be achieved to perform a miracle.

One is reminded of the psychic surgeons of the Philippines, who seem to penetrate a patient's body with their hands and pull out all manner of bloody tissue, none of it anything that would be seen inside a body at autopsy. In many cases patients report that they can actually feel the surgeon's fingers, and dramatic recoveries have been reported.

In quantum terms we can offer an explanation for what medicine men are accomplishing on the outskirts of the miraculous. As we know from our quantum model, any object can be reduced to packets of energy.

At the level of ordinary life, the events remain baffling, hence the widespread skepticism over holy apparitions, psychic surgeons, and jungle medicine men. But the visionary response describes another level of consciousness where energy patterns are shifting with every thought. The fact that these shifts change the outer world is amazing to us but natural to the person in stage six.

Who am I? . . .
Enlightened awareness.

Starting with the physical body in stage one and steadily moving to less physical planes, now we arrive at nothing but awareness. My identity floats in a quantum fog as photons wink in and out of existence.

Of the million ways you could define enlightenment, identifying with the light is a good one. Jesus spoke in parables but could easily have been literal when he declared to his disciples, "You are the light of the world."

From the larger perspective, no one has the power to keep God out totally. We can only open or close our acceptance of the light.

Things are real in the quantum world if you *make* them real, and that is done by manipulating light. With care and patience, anyone can be taught to do that; healing touch is only one mode.

How do I fit in? . . .
I love.

When he realizes that he is bathed in light, the feeling that comes over a miracle worker is one of intense love. When Jesus said "I am the light," he meant "I'm totally in God's force field."

We are all in the force field of love, but in early stages of spiritual growth, its power is weak. We waver and can easily be thrown off in other directions. Only after years of cleaning out the inner blockages of repression, doubt, negative emotions, and old conditioning does a person realize that God's force is immensely powerful. When this occurs, nothing can pull the mind away from love. Love as a personal emotion is transmuted into a cosmic energy.

It takes a quantum leap in consciousness to love God all the time, yet when the leap is finally made, there is really no God to love, not as a separate object. The fusion of the worshiper and what he worships is nearly complete. But that is enough to animate everything in creation.

How do I find God? . . .
Grace.

Sometimes God is felt with ecstasy, but just as often there can be pain, anguish, and confusion. This mixture of feelings reminds us that two entities are coming into conjunction. One is spirit, the other is body.

In another sense, though, grace offers constant support in everyday life.

If God is like a force field in stage six, grace is his magnetic pull. Grace adapts itself to each person. We make our choices, some of which are good for us, some bad, and then grace shapes the results.

When you feel you have been touched by grace, that is your clue that God exists and cares about what happens to you.

Whether operating on the level of a saint or a criminal, grace is the ingredient that saves karma from being heartlessly mechanical. A billiard ball must follow its assigned trajectory, and a thief who commits robbery a hundred times would seem to be just as set on his course. But at any given moment he has the opportunity to stop and mend his ways. The impulse to move toward spirit is the result of grace.

What is the nature of good and evil? . . .
Good is a cosmic force.
Evil is another aspect of the same force.

It is so difficult to be good that eventually a person must give up. This is a realization that arrives in stage six. In Christianity this struggle is predestined to end with the victory of good, since God is more powerful than Satan, but in Hinduism the forces of light and darkness will battle eternally.

In stage six a person is visionary enough to see this. He still retains a conception of good. It is the force of evolution that lies behind birth, growth, love, truth, and beauty. He also retains a conception of evil. It is the force that opposes evolution—we would call it entropy—leading to decomposition, dissolution, inertia, and "sin" (in the special sense of any action that doesn't help a person's evolution). However, to the visionary these are two sides of the same force. God created both because both are needed; God is in the evil as much as in the good.

What is my life challenge? . . .
To attain liberation.

When stage six dawns, the purpose of life changes. Instead of striving for goodness and virtue, the person aims to escape bondage. God's force field, as we have been calling it, exerts an attraction to pull the soul out of the range of karma. The most enlightened saint still has a physical body subject to decay and death; he still eats, drinks, and sleeps. However, all of this energy gets used in a different way.

Good deeds have their own rewards, just as bad deeds do. What if you don't want any reward at all but just to be free? This is the state Buddhists call nirvana, much misunderstood when it is translated as "oblivion."

Nirvana is the release from karmic influences, the end of the dance of opposites.

Since only God is free from cause and effect, to want nirvana means that you want to attain God-realization. For the sake of keeping society together, religions hold it as a duty to respect goodness and abhor evil. How can God want us to be good and yet want us to go beyond good?

The answer takes place entirely in consciousness.

In stage six the alchemy of turning evil into a blessing is a mystery that is solved by longing for liberation.

What is my greatest temptation? . . .
Martyrdom.

Are saints tempted to turn into martyrs?

In early Christianity, dying for the faith became exalted as imitation of Christ.

I am not denigrating martyrdom here, but it is worth pointing out that stage six is not the end of the journey, not quite yet. As long as suffering holds any temptation, there is some hint of sin, and in that arises the last tiny separation between God and the devotee. The ego retains enough power to say that "I" am proving my holiness to God. In the next stage there will be nothing left to prove and therefore no "I" at all. Getting to that point is the last struggle of the saint. By the smallest hair there is a distance to go. Amazingly, in that fraction of distance an entire world will be created.

STAGE SEVEN:
GOD OF PURE BEING — "I AM"
(Sacred Response)

There is a God who can only be experienced by going beyond experience.

The God of stage seven is known when all else is forgotten. Each person is tied to the world by a thousand invisible threads of mental activity—time, place, identity, and all past experiences. When you think you know something, you refer only to some scrap of the past.

As my mind revolves and buzzes with this data, it keeps assuring me that I am real. Why do I need this assurance? No one asks this question as long as the world is with us.

In place of the highest ecstasy, one gets emptiness. The God of stage seven is so intangible that he can be defined by no qualities. Nothing remains to hold on to.

The empty void contains the potential for all life and all experience.

The mystery of stage seven is that nothingness can mask infinity.

You have to climb the spiritual ladder from one rung to the next. Now that we are high enough to view the whole landscape, it's time to kick the ladder away. No support at all, not even the mind, is needed.

Everything around us is the product of who we are. In stage seven you no longer project God; you project everything, which is the same as being in the movie, outside the movie, and the movie itself. In unity consciousness no separation is left. We no longer create God in our image, not even the faintest image of a holy ghost.

Who am I? . . .
The source.

A person who reaches stage seven is so free of attachment that if you ask, "Who are you?" the only answer is: "I am."

At the virtual level there is no energy, time, or space. This apparent void, however, is the source of everything measurable as energy, time, and space, just as a blank mind is the source of all thoughts.

In stage seven two impossible things must converge. The person has to be reduced to the merest point, a speck of identity closing the last minuscule gap between himself and God. At the same time, just when separation is healed, the tiny point has to expand to infinity. The mystics describe this as "the One becomes All." To put it into scientific terms, when you cross into the quantum zone, space-time collapses into itself. The tiniest thing in existence merges with the greatest; point and infinity are equal.

The process really does sound like dying, because no matter how you approach it, one must give up the known world to attain stage seven.

The spiritual journey takes you to the place where you began as a soul, a mere point of consciousness, naked and undressed of qualities. This source is yourself.

It doesn't wipe out ordinary existence—you still eat, drink, walk, and act out desires. But now the desires do not belong to anyone; they are remnants of who you used to be.

Karma means always wanting more of what won't get you anywhere in the first place. In stage seven you realize this and no longer chase after phantoms. Now you end up at the source, which is pure being.

How do I fit in? . . .
I am.

Once the adventure of soul-searching is over, things calm down.

The smallest irritants and the greatest tragedies, a pebble in your shoe and World War II, become equally unreal.

The end of illusion is the end of experience as we know it. What do you receive in exchange? Only reality, pure and unvarnished.

In stage seven there is a shift of balance; one starts to notice the unchanging much more than the changing. Stage seven isn't a prize or reward for making right choices; it is the realization of what you always have been.

How do I find God? . . .
By transcending.

Transcending is going beyond. In spiritual terms it also means growing up. "When I was no longer a child, I put aside childish things," writes Saint Paul. By analogy, even karma can be outgrown and put aside. Two ultimate realities vie for our approval. One is karma, the reality of actions and desires. The other reality that claims to be ultimate has no action in it; it just is.

However, to see yourself caught between two choices is false.

The reason, then, to return to the source derives from self-interest. I don't want to be bored; I don't want to come to the end of the chase and wind up empty-handed. Here all metaphors and analogies end, because just as a dream gets exposed as illusion when you wake up, so Being eventually unmasks karma.

At its source, the cosmos is equally real and unreal. The only way I have of knowing anything is through the neurons firing in my brain, and although I could see every photon inside my cortex, at that point the cortex dissolves into photons as well. So the observer and the thing he is trying to observe merge, which is exactly how the chase after God also ends.

What is the nature of good and evil? . . .
Good is the union of all opposites.
Evil no longer exists.

Only when it is totally absorbed into unity does the threat of evil end once and for all.

A gap that keeps us from imagining how all fear, temptation, sin, evil, and imperfection is transcended.

History comes to an end here on earth when Satan is accepted back into heaven; then the triumph of God becomes complete.

We all equate pain with evil, and as a sensation, pain doesn't end; it is part of our biological inheritance. The only way to get beyond it is to transcend. In stage seven all versions of the world are seen as projections, and a projection is nothing more than a point of view that has come to life. The highest point of view, then, would encompass anything that happens, without preference and without rejection.

In stage seven a person realizes that it isn't up to us to balance the scales; if we hand our choices over to God, we are free to act as the impulse moves us, knowing its source is divine unity.

What is my life challenge? . . .
To be myself.

Nothing would seem easier than to be yourself, but people complain endlessly about how hard it is. Once society has imposed its demands, freedom is more restricted still. Alone on a desert island you might be able to be yourself, only guilt and shame would pursue you even there. The inheritance of repression is inescapable.

The whole problem is one of boundaries and resistance. Unless someone tells me what I can't do, I have nothing to push against. By implication, my life would be shapeless. I would follow one whim after another, which itself is a kind of prison.

In stage seven the problem comes to an end as boundaries and resistance both melt. To be in unity, you cannot have limitations. You are wholeness; that is what fills your perception. Choice A and choice B are equal in your eyes. Being myself no longer has the slightest outside reference.

Before stage seven the full value of being yourself isn't known. Every divine image remains an image; every vision tempts us to hold on to it. To be really free, there is no option except to be yourself. You are the living center around which every event happens, yet no event is so important that you willingly give yourself up to it. In this way life remains fresh and fulfills its need to renew itself at every moment.

What is my greatest strength? . . .
Unity.

What is my biggest hurdle? . . .
Duality.

The opposite of unity is duality. Currently two dominant versions of reality are believed by almost everyone. Version one: there is only the material world, and nothing can be real that doesn't obey physical laws. Version two: two realities exist, the earthly and the divine.

Version one is called the secular view, and even religious people adopt it for everyday use. Yet total belief in materialism, as we have seen, has become unacceptable for a host of reasons. It cannot explain credible, witnessed miracles, near-death experiences, out-of-body experiences, the testimony of millions of people who have had answered prayers, and most convincing of all, the discovery of the quantum world, which doesn't obey any ordinary physical laws.

The second version of reality is less rigid. It allows

for spiritual experience and miracles, which exist on the fringes of the material world. At this moment someone is hearing the voice of God, witnessing the Virgin Mary, or going into the light. These experiences still leave the material world intact and essentially untouched. You can have God and a Mercedes at the same time, each on its own level. In other words, there is duality.

In India there has been a strong nondual tradition for thousands of years, known as Vedanta. The word literally means "the end of the Vedas," the point where no sacred texts can help you anymore, where teaching stops and awareness dawns.

The main tenet of Vedanta is extremely simple— duality is too weak to stand forever. Take any sin or delusion, and in time it will come to an end. Take any pleasure, and in time it will start to pall. In Vedanta they say that the only real thing is eternal bliss consciousness *(sat chit ananda)*. These words promise that the timeless waits for me when the temporary expires, bliss outlives pleasure, and being awake comes after sleep. In that simplicity the whole notion of duality collapses, revealing the unity behind all illusion.

What is my greatest temptation? . . .
Beyond temptation.

You can't be tempted when you have it all. It is even better when they can't take it away from you. It is the power of existence. You have it forever when you can say, "I am that power, you are that power, and everything around us is that power."

The sage Vasishtha was one of the first human beings to realize that we experience only the world we filter through our minds. Whatever I can imagine is a product of my life experience so far, and that is the tiniest fragment of what I could know. As Vasishtha himself wrote:

> *Infinite worlds come and go*
> *in the vast expanse of consciousness,*
> *like motes of dust dancing in a beam of light.*

This is a reminder that if the material world is just a product of my awareness, so is heaven. I have every right, therefore, to try to know the mind of God. A journey that begins in mystery and silence ends with myself.

4

A MANUAL FOR SAINTS

We are like newborn children,
Our power is the power to grow.
— RABINDRANATH TAGORE

WHEN YOU READ ABOUT THE SEVEN STAGES, IT
becomes clear that religions vary wildly on how to
know God. Each has marked out a separate path
whose steps are fixed—often rigidly fixed—in
dogma.

Yet every religious tradition has saints. Saints are
spiritual achievers. They exhibit deep love and devotion, but saints are more than saintly. Since saints
begin life the same as the rest of us, developing a natural sense of love, forgiveness, and compassion repre-

sents a huge accomplishment. Not only have they reached the spiritual goals set forth by their religion, but they prove to the rest of us that the resources exist for getting there ourselves.

This implies that the saint is laying out a map of the future. The saints of Buddhism, who are called bodhisattvas, are sometimes portrayed looking over their shoulders and beckoning with a smile, as if to say, "I am going over the threshold. Don't you want to follow?"

It makes sense to accept their invitation, not just by showing love and compassion, but by heeding the principles that uphold the soul's journey. These principles would be found in any manual for saints because they hold true from stage one to stage seven. Such a manual doesn't exist, but if it did, the following realizations would be right at its core:

> *Evolution cannot be stopped; spiritual growth is assured.*
>
> *Action is always noticed by God; nothing goes unheeded.*
>
> *There is no reliable guide to behavior outside your own heart and mind.*
>
> *Reality changes at different stages of growth.*
>
> *At some level everyone knows the highest truth.*

Everyone is doing the best they can from their own level of consciousness.

Suffering is temporary, enlightenment is forever.

These realizations come from paying attention to the countless clues left by spirit. No two people see God in the same way, because no two people are at the exact same stage of waking up. Yet in those moments when the five senses give way to deeper intuition, each of us gets a glimpse of reality, and as our minds process some remarkable event or insight, reality delivers a scrap of truth.

To judge by the outer show, everyone's life moves rapidly, if chaotically, through scene after scene. Yet you might never suspect that there even was an inner journey. Saints prove that there is. Having arrived at the goal, they can look back and say that just beneath the surface, human life has a pattern, a rising arc.

The road to sainthood begins in ordinary circumstances with ordinary situations. There is no shorter path to God. Because we all have egos, we fantasize that we will simply leap to the top of the mountain where the halos are handed out, but this never happens. Inner life is too complex, too full of contradictions. In spiritual exploration the map shifts with every step you take.

Which brings us back to the same question, "Where do I go from here?"

The rising arc of spirit isn't always obvious. It gets obscured all the time. We don't think about sainthood when corporate downsizing threatens our jobs or when the divorce papers are served. But at dramatic moments the soul drops clues into our laps, and then we have the choice to pay attention or not. Your soul will always be in communication with you, and over time you will heed what it says.

That is why it is useful to cooperate in your own awakening—your enemy is not evil but lack of attention. The various practices known as prayer, meditation, contemplation, and yoga have been highly valued over the centuries because they sharpen attention and make it easier not to miss the clues to spiritual reality.

A spiritual person is a good listener for the inner voice that plays its beliefs over and over in your head until you move on to a new belief, bringing with it a new voice.

The saint sees that we are all hooked into the same level of infinite intelligence, creativity, and love. God and your soul are in perfect communication. The message breaks down for reasons we have been detailing at length: ego needs, distortions of perception, lack of self-worth, and all kinds of traumas and wounds that defeat our best intentions. By not knowing who we are, by not knowing what God is, by not knowing how to connect with the soul, we fall into sin and ignorance. In everyday usage, avidya is sometimes called both sin and ignorance, but these pejorative terms hide the essence of the truth, which is that all such obstacles exist in consciousness and can be cleared away.

What's the one thing you can do today to grow in spirit? Stop defining yourself. Don't accept any thought that begins "I am this or that." You are not this or that. You are beyond definition, and therefore any attempt to say "I am X" is wrong. You are in the process of redefining yourself every day. Aid that process, and you cannot help but leap forward on the path.

It takes a lot of attention to look in the mirror, because our masks do not stop looking back at us. But if you take any issue facing you, your present attitudes will be a clue to your deeper beliefs, and belief is where the real change must occur. A belief is like a microchip that keeps sending out the same signal over and over, making the same interpretation of reality until you are ready to pull out the old chip and install a new one.

As a child I felt left out spiritually because I would never meet Buddha or Krishna, and my eyes would never see someone raised from the dead or water turned to wine. Now I realize that it isn't the miracle that creates the believer. Instead, we are all believers. We believe that the illusion of the material world is completely real. That belief is our only prison. It prevents us from making the journey into the unknown. To date, after many centuries of saints, sages, and seers, only a few individuals can open to radical change in their belief system, while most cannot. Even so, our beliefs must eventually shift to conform to reality, since in the quantum world, belief creates reality. As we will see, our true home is the light, and our true role is to create endlessly from the infinite storehouse of possibilities located at the virtual level.

5

STRANGE POWERS

. . . for all things are possible with God.

— MARK 10:27

IF THERE ARE TWO REALITIES COMPETING FOR our allegiance, the material and the spiritual, why should we abandon the material? Since God doesn't interfere to bring even the bare necessities to millions of poor people, disbelief makes sense.

Yet disbelief doesn't seem to work, either. There are mysterious phenomena that can be explained only in terms of an invisible domain that is our source in the sacred. It is the home of our intelligence and our sense of order in the universe. To prove that such a place exists, we look to a vast range of anomalies on the fringes of ordinary events. These include religious awakening and "going into the light," which we have already covered, but also the following:

Inspiration and insight

Geniuses, child prodigies, and savants

Memory of former lifetimes

Telepathy and ESP

Alter egos (multiple personality syndrome)

Synchronicity

Clairvoyance and prophecy

Diverse as they are, these fringe phenomena all take us beyond our present knowledge of the brain into the regions of the "mind field" that are closest to God. The brain is a receiver of mind, like a radio receiving signals from a faraway source.

We will be working on this connection in the following sections, and as we do it will become clearer that quantum reality—the zone of miracles—is a place very nearby.

INSPIRATION AND INSIGHT

When you feel inspired, more than ordinary thinking is involved. There is a sense of being uplifted, of suddenly breaking through. Old boundaries fall away, and one feels, if only for a moment, a rush of liberation. If the inspiration is powerful enough, one's whole life can be changed. There are insights so potent that years of patterned behavior can change in an instant.

I believe that life events do not unfold randomly; our materialistic worldview may insist that they do, but all of us have reflected on turning points in our lives and seen, sometimes with bafflement or wonder, that lessons came our way at exactly the time we needed them.

In a word, some hidden intelligence seems to know when and how to transform us, often when we least expect it. By its nature, inspiration is transforming—it brings in spirit—and no model of the brain has come close to explaining how a cluster of neurons could transform itself.

Inspiration is the perfect example of how the invisible level of reality works. *Whatever is needed is provided.* Your mind isn't a computer; it is a living intelligence, and it evolves, which is why fresh insight is needed.

In the primitive stages of evolution, the leap from algae to plants was a leap of intelligence, a moment of inspiration, just as much as the discovery of relativity.

At every level, to be inspired is a step toward greater liberation, and liberation is a choice.

In the domain of the mind there is both freedom and attachment; we make the choice which to attune to. Each person sets his own boundaries and breaks through them when the evolutionary impulse is felt.

We've all met people whose problems are completely unnecessary, yet they lack the insight to find the solution. Try to give them this insight, hand it to them on a platter, and still they won't take it. Insight and inspiration must be sought and then allowed to dawn. As our spiritual masters indicate, this is the kind of knowledge you must tune into. Inspiration teaches us that transformation must begin with trust that a higher intelligence exists and knows how to contact us.

MEMORY OF FORMER LIFETIMES

Who were you before you were you? The possibility of an afterlife is widely argued in the West, but the existence of a before-life is just as likely. If you believe only in an afterlife, you are restricted to a very limited, dualistic view of time. There is only "here" and "after." But if life is continuous, if the soul never stops making its journey, a completely different worldview opens up.

People who spend time with geniuses and prodigies often find them unearthly, somehow preternatural, as if a very old soul has been confined to a new body and yet brings in experience far beyond what that body could have known. It is easy to credit that some kind of former life is casting its influence on the present.

The unmanifest domain allows us to see this issue a different way. We can frame the notion of former lives as one of awareness. It would seem that the mind isn't limited by experience—all of us have had moments when we know much more than we should.

There is much evidence that the mind is not confined by time and space.

DNA is composed of simple sugars and bits of protein that never divide or reproduce, no matter how many billions of years they exist. What step caused these simple molecules to get together, arrange themselves in a pattern with billions of tiny segments, and all of a sudden learn to divide?

One plausible answer is that an invisible organizing principle is at work. The need for life to reproduce itself is fundamental; the need for chemicals to reproduce themselves is nil. So even at this most basic level, we see certain qualities of awareness—recognition, memory, self-preservation, and identity—coming into play. Now add the element of time.

To form a baby, a single fertilized cell must be a master of timing. Every organ of the body exists in seed form within a single strand of DNA, yet to emerge correctly, they must take their turn. For the first days and weeks, an embryo is called a zygote or seed; it is an undifferentiated mass of similar cells. But very soon one cell starts to give off chemicals unique to itself. Even though the mother cells are identical, some of the offspring know, for example, that they are meant to be brain cells. As such, they need to specialize, growing into far different shapes than muscle or bone cells. This they do with amazing precision, but in addition they send out signals to attract other proto-brain cells. Like attracts like, and as brain cells float toward each other, they cross paths with proto-heart, proto-kidney, and proto-stomach cells, none of them getting in the way or causing a confusion of identity.

This spectacle is far more astonishing than the eye can see. Think of it: a baby brain cell somehow knows who it is going to be in advance. How does it keep track of its purpose in life with so many billions of signals being sent all around it? Memory, learning, and identity precede matter; they govern matter.

I conclude that the field of awareness is our true home, and that awareness contains the secrets of evolution, not the body or even DNA.

Now let's return to the original question: Who were you before you were you? The Vedic seers say, "The real you cannot be squeezed into the volume of a body or the span of a lifetime." Just as reality flows from the virtual to the quantum to the material level, so do you. Whether we call this reincarnation or not almost doesn't matter. This is how a single fertilized cell learns to become a brain—it wakes up to itself, not on the chemical level but on the level of awareness.

Now imagine that expanded awareness is normal. Time and space could just be convenient concepts that hold true in the material world but dissolve gradually as you approach the quantum level. This is what I believe reincarnation is about. Former lives fall into the unexplored territory of expanded awareness. It isn't absolutely necessary to decide whether they are "real" or not. Concrete verification that I was a Nepalese soldier at the time of the Emperor Ashoka is never going to come my way. But if I find myself extremely attracted to that period, if I start to read about Ashoka and his conversion to Buddhism, and if my empathy is so strong that I cannot help but adopt some of those principles, we can truthfully say that a wider range of life has influenced my mind. In a very real sense, the terms *former life* and *expanded life* are the same thing.

People who shut out their former lives—if we want to use that terminology—are shutting out lessons that give this present lifetime its purpose and meaning. For someone who has absorbed these lessons fully, there is no need to go beyond this lifetime.

Finally, the fact that we are not confined to our physical body and mind gives us reason to believe in the existence of a cosmic intelligence that permeates life.

The timeless place where God exists can't be reduced to an address. Our exploration into former lifetimes indicates that the same may be true of us as well.

CLAIRVOYANCE AND PROPHECY

As we have seen, the things that seem so well defined in the material world turn into shadowy phantoms the deeper we go into the unmanifest domain. Time is no exception, and at a certain level of reality it hardly exists. When the boundary of time dissolves completely, it is possible to experience a kind of mental time travel called clairvoyance, or the ability to see into the future.

The clairvoyant is experiencing an "unreal" visual state, yet the inner vision happens to come true. How, then, can a purely internal firing of neurons match events that have not come to pass?

I know of clairvoyants who give accurate images of a future mate or the outcome of a lawsuit, down to the exact timing of a judge's rulings. This accuracy gives serious pause. It implies that there is more than one way for the future to flow into the present.

There are no definite events, no river of time that flows from past to present to future. What exists are infinite choices within every event, and we determine which select few are going to manifest. We may be choosing not to be clairvoyant so that our belief in a hidden future is confirmed.

In the clairvoyant vision, the future has two locations—here and later. He can choose which one to participate in.

Those of us who accept a simpler world, in which the future has only one location—later—are showing a personal preference; we are not obeying an iron law. Time dictates that first one thing happens and then the next, without overlap. You cannot be a child and an adult simultaneously—except through clairvoyance. Then the leaking of one event into the next is allowed.

In general, the highest purpose of clairvoyance may be to give us a glimpse into the mind of God, because a divine mind could not be constrained by time and does not recognize past, present, or future. This is the ultimate mystery of clairvoyance—any moment, whether now or later, is a doorway into eternity.

I believe that prophets live in this expanded space as well.

We can begin to understand how this works only by our knowledge of quantum reality, for there all light is born. Energy is not separate from space-time.

They form one tapestry. The astrologer goes a step further. He breaks the entire cosmos down into specific kinds of energy as they apply to human existence.

The concept of information embedded in energy isn't totally alien outside astrology. To a physicist information is pervasive throughout nature. The specific frequencies that make infrared light different from ultraviolet, or gamma rays different from radio waves, all form a kind of cosmic code. It is the information embedded in energy that allows us to build electrical generators, infrared lamps, radio beacons, and so forth. Without that coded information, the universe would be a random vibration.

To be able to cross the boundary of time or to speak the language of light tells us that even our most basic assumptions are open to choice. Awareness is all. The past and the future are distractions, pulling us into an abstract mental state that will never be alive. Once awareness is willing to expand, you can dive infinitely into this moment. If we experience our minds as multidimensional, we get closer to God's mind, which is all-dimensional.

6

CONTACTING GOD

Ask, and it will be given to you; seek, and you will find;
knock, and it will be opened to you.

— MATTHEW 7:7

KNOWING GOD WOULD BE IMPOSSIBLE IF HE
didn't want to be known. There is nothing to prevent
every stage of spirituality from being a delusion. The
saint who speaks to God may be suffering from a le-
sion of the right temporal lobe. On the other hand, a
convinced atheist may be shutting out messages from
God every day.

Our quantum model tells us three ways that God
is already contacting us:

1.   He exists at a level of reality beyond the five senses that is the source of our being. Since we are quantum creatures, we participate in God all the time without acknowledging it.

2.   He is sending us messages or clues into the physical world.

3.   He is attracting notice through "second attention," the deepest intuitive part of our brains, which most people ignore.

These three ways to know God are based on the facts accumulated in our search so far. We've built the plane and we know the theory of flight—what remains is to take off.

God seems to be sending us messages from outside time and space. Some of these spiritual clues are faint, but some are very dramatic. One of the most recent healings at Lourdes happened to a young Irishman afflicted with multiple sclerosis. He arrived late at the shrine, after the holy waters were closed.

Disappointed, he was taken back to his hotel in a wheelchair. Sitting alone in his room, he suddenly felt a change. A bolt of light shot up his spine, causing him to writhe from its intensity; he lost consciousness. But when he awoke, he could walk, and all signs of his MS had vanished. He returned home healed. I think there is no doubt, given the thousands of people who have had such experiences, that this is the "light of God," revered in every sacred tradition. God enters our world in few other ways that are as tangible.

To get back to the source of God's messages, we would have to use second attention, our ability to know something without any physical information. Intuition and prophecy involve second attention. So does the saint's insight into God.

By seeking to know God we run into the same problem we do when we seek to know what lies outside the universe.

Without ever seeing into this other world, we can observe black holes and quasars, which are the nearest thing to windows on the edge of infinity. As light and energy get sucked into a black hole, they disappear from our cosmos. This implies that they are going somewhere; therefore they might also return to us via "white holes" or acts of creation like the Big Bang. God is not this knowable, however.

To know God personally, you must penetrate a boundary that physicists call "the event horizon," a line that divides reality sharply in half. On this side lies anything that remains within the speed of light; on the other side is anything faster than the speed of light. The speed of light is absolute; it is like a wall that no object can crash through. As we approach the wall, time slows down, mass increases, and space becomes curved. If you try to crash through, weird things happen to prevent you from doing so.

For example, any light that passes too near a black hole gets pulled into its field of gravity. Black holes are the remnants of old stars that collapsed onto themselves. In some instances the momentum is irreversible, and even light cannot escape from the star's force field. In that case there is only blackness. If a photon of light tries to go around a black hole, it will start to curve in the hole's direction until it falls in.

To an outside observer, the photon falls into the back hole forever, frozen in time. Inside the black hole, however, the photon has already been devoured. Both versions are true. One is seen from the world of light, the other from the world beyond light. This borderline of uncertainty is the event horizon, the exact margin dividing reality in half between the certain and the uncertain, the known and the unknown.

Any place where knowledge stops there is also an event horizon. The brain can't explore beyond where photons go. What lies beyond the event horizon? It could be a new universe with intelligent life in it; or it could be a chaos of squashed dimensions tumbling like twisted sheets in a dryer.

Quantum physics dips across the border all the time, only it can't stay there very long. When a particle accelerator bombards two atoms, causing a subatomic particle to jump out of its hiding place for a few millionths of a second, the event horizon has been crossed. Science inched its way toward nuclear power, transistors, and (if we look into the future) advanced computer memory and time travel. Already a beam of light has been made to move from one location to another in a Cal Tech laboratory without crossing the space in between, which is a form of primitive time travel.

What we do know is that God can't be on this side of the event horizon. Since the Big Bang, light has been traveling for about ten to fifteen billion years. Strangely enough, certain faraway objects appear to be emitting radiation that is older than the universe, a fact cosmologists are unable to comprehend. If the human brain contains its own event horizon (the limit of photons to organize themselves as thought) and so does the cosmos, we must cross over to find the home of spirit.

A MAP OF THE SOUL

In the ancient Vedas it says that the part of us that doesn't believe in death will never die. This simple definition of the soul is not a bad one. It accurately describes everyone's secret belief that death may be real for some but not for us. Psychologists are impatient with this feeling of personal immortality. They claim that we use it to defend ourselves against the inescapable fact that one day we will die. But what if the opposite is true? What if feeling immortal and beyond death is the most real thing about us?

To prove this point one way or another, we need facts, just as we needed them about God. The soul is as mysterious as God, and we have just as few reliable facts about it. I would offer that the first fact about the soul is that it is not really as personal as people believe. The soul doesn't feel or move; it doesn't travel with you as you go about your life, nor does it endure birth, decay, and death. This is just a way of saying that the soul stands apart from ordinary experience. Since it also has no shape, getting a mental picture of the soul isn't possible.

In India the soul has two parts. One is called *Jiva,* which corresponds to the individual soul making its long journey through many lifetimes until it reaches full realization of God. When a child is taught that being good means your soul will go to heaven, it is Jiva that we are talking about. Jiva is involved in action. It is affected by our good and bad acts; it rules our conscience, and all the seeds of karma are planted inside it. The kind of person you turn out to be is rooted in Jiva, and the kind of life you make for yourself will change Jiva day by day.

The second half of the soul, called *Atman,* does not accompany us on any journey. It is pure spirit, made of the same essence as God. Atman cannot change in any way. It never reaches God because it never left in the first place. No matter how good or bad your life, your Atman remains constant; in fact, the worst criminal and the holiest saint have the same quality of soul when it is this aspect that is in question. There is no good approximation for Atman in the West, and many people might wonder why the soul has to be divided in this way.

We have seen that all the familiar qualities of life, such as time, space, energy, and matter, gradually fade into a shadowy existence until they disappear. But this disappearance leaves something intact—spirit itself. Jiva lives at the quantum level, Atman at the virtual. So the faintest, subtlest trace of "me" that can be detected at the quantum level is Jiva, and once it disappears, pure spirit remains—that is Atman. The distinction between them is absolutely necessary, for otherwise the path back to God would break down.

As you can see, even though they are melded together as "soul," these two aspects are exact opposites in many ways. Such is the paradox of the soul that it manages to accommodate itself to our world of time, thought, and action while dwelling eternally in the spiritual world. The soul must be half-human, half-divine in order to give us a way to retain our identity during all the prayer, meditation, seeking, and other spiritual work that is involved in finding God, and yet the soul must have a divine aspect that embodies the goal of all seeking.

On the material level I am not aware of my Atman. I walk and talk and think without any consciousness that my source lies much deeper. But at the soul level I am totally aware of who I am. The soul level is a very strange place, because it gives rise to all activity without being active itself. Think about that carefully. As I travel around from here to there, my soul doesn't move, because at the quantum level the field just ripples and vibrates—it doesn't change location from A to B. I am born, grow old, and die—these events have tremendous significance for my body and mind. Yet at the quantum level nothing is born, grows old, or dies. There is no such thing as an old photon.

To a quantum physicist, our bodies are just objects, like any other. A ball thrown across the room isn't moving, only winking in and out of existence at an incredibly fast speed at different locations, and we are no different. But here the mystery deepens. When the ball disappears for a nanosecond, only to reappear just the tiniest bit to the left or right, why didn't it disintegrate? After all, it was completely absent for a while, and there is no reason why its old shape and size and color shouldn't simply dissolve. Quantum physics can even calculate the odds that it won't reappear, that instead of a ball flying across the room, a bowl of pink Jell-O will suddenly appear. What keeps things together?

This is essentially the argument for the soul. It holds reality together; it is my offscreen director, my presiding intelligence. I can think, talk, work, love, and dream, all because of the soul, yet the soul doesn't do any of these things. It is me, yet I would never recognize it if we came face-to-face. Everything that makes the difference between life and death must cross into this world via the soul.

THE POWER OF INTENTION

The aim of spirituality is to learn to cooperate with God. Most of us have been raised to do the opposite. Our skills and abilities come from first attention and not second. As a result, our issues tend to center on the lower stages, where fear and neediness, however much we deny them, take their toll. In these early stages the ego asserts its needs with great force—money, security, sex, and power make huge claims on everyone in society. It is important to realize that God doesn't judge against these things—when people feel that they owe their success to God, they are right. When wrongdoing goes unpunished and good deeds are ignored, God smiles on both. There is only one reality, which is spiritual, and nothing lies outside God's mind. We tap into the source of creativity and intelligence with every thought.

What makes a life spiritual, then?

The difference is entirely one of intention. I began this book by saying that two people could be followed around from birth to death with a camera, and there would be no external way to show which one believed in God. This fact remains true. Unless you become a recluse or enter a monastery, your social role is irrelevant to how spiritual you are. Everything depends on intention. If someone uses kind words but intends to snub you, the intention cuts through. The most expensive gift cannot make up for lack of love. We know instinctively when intentions come from an honest place or a place of deception.

In spiritual life, intention includes will and purpose, aspiration and highest vision. If you set your intention toward God, spirit grows. If you set your intention toward material existence, that will grow instead. Once you plant the seed of an intention, your soul's journey unfolds automatically. Here are the basic intentions that mark a spiritual life, stated in terms of what a person wants to achieve:

- *I want to feel God's presence.* This intention is rooted in the discomfort of being isolated and separate. When God is absent, the underlying feeling of loneliness cannot be escaped. You can mask it by developing friendships and family ties. Ultimately, however, each of us needs to feel a sense of inner fullness and peace. We want to be satisfied within ourselves, no matter if we are alone or in a crowd.

- *I want God to aid and support me.* God's presence brings with it the qualities of spirit. At the source, every quality—love, intelligence, truth, organizing ability, creativity—becomes infinite. The growth of these things in your life is a sign that you are approaching closer to your soul.

- *I want to feel connected to the whole.* The soul's journey takes a person from a fragmented state to a state of wholeness. This is felt as being more connected. Events around you start to weave into a pattern. Small details fit together instead of being scattered and random.

- *I want my life to have meaning.* Existence feels empty in separation, and this gets healed only by moving into unity with God. Instead of turning outward to find your purpose, you feel that just being here, as you are, fulfills the highest purpose in creation.

- *I want to be free of restrictions.* Inner freedom is greatly compromised when fear is present, and fear is a natural outcome of separation. As you move closer to your soul, the old boundaries and defenses start to melt away. Instead of being wary about the future, you flow with the river of life, awaiting the day when no boundaries of any kind hold you back.

If these basic intentions are present inside you, God takes the responsibility for carrying them out. Everything else you do is secondary. Someone who is in the grip of fear, for example, cannot move beyond stage one, despite good deeds, a secure home life, and positive thinking. We all attempt to mask our limitations with false attitudes; it is only human nature to try to appear better than we are, especially in our own eyes. But once you set your intention in the right direction, self-deception is rendered irrelevant. You will still have to face your ego needs; you will still continue to play out your personal dramas. This activity takes place on the stage of first attention; offstage, spirit has its own devices—your intention is like a blueprint handed to God, which he carries to completion in his own fashion. Sometimes he uses a miracle; sometimes he just makes sure you don't miss the plane to New York. The fact that anything can happen is the beauty and surprise of the spiritual life.

Strangely, people who feel extremely powerful and successful often set the worst intentions in motion, as far as spiritual growth is concerned. Here are some typical intentions that have nothing to do with finding God:

I want to win.
I want to prove myself by taking risks.

I want to have power over others.
I want to make the rules.
I want to be in control.
I want to do it all my way.

These intentions should sound very familiar since they are repeated ad nauseam in popular fiction, advertising, and the media. They all center on ego needs, and as long as your real intentions come from that level, your life will follow suit. Such is the fate of living in a mirror universe. One meets hundreds of people who mistake their own intentions because their egos have taken complete control. Some of the most powerful figures in the world are spiritually quite naive. If intention is left to the ego, great things can be accomplished, but these are minuscule compared to what can be achieved with infinite intelligence and organizing power at your disposal.

God is on the side of abundance. It is a great misfortune that the spiritual life has earned a reputation for being poor, reclusive, and ascetic. God is also on the side of increased happiness. The shadow of the martyr has fallen over spirituality with dire results. In general, to be spiritual in these times means going it alone, far more than in the past. In a society with misguided conceptions of God and no tradition of masters, you are responsible for setting your own intentions.

Here are the ground rules that have proved effective for me personally and which I feel will work for many people:

1. **Know your intentions.** Look at the list of spiritual intentions above and make sure that you understand how important they are. Your destiny is to move in the direction of your soul, but the fuel that makes destiny move is intention. Intend for yourself that the gap of separation gets closed just a little more each day. Don't let your false intentions remain masked. Root them out and work on the anger and fear that keep you attached to them. False intentions take the form of guilty desires: I want someone else to fail, I want to get even, I want to see bad people punished, I want to take away something not my own. False intentions can be elusive; you will notice their existence by the feeling tone connected with them, a feeling of fear, greed, rage, hopelessness, and weakness. Sense the feeling first, refuse to buy into it, and then remain aware until you find the intention lurking beneath.

2. **Set your intentions high.** Aim to be a saint and a miracle worker. Why not? The same laws of nature operate for everyone. If you know that the goal of inner growth is to acquire mastery, then ask for that mastery as soon as possible. Once you ask, don't strain to work wonders, but don't deny them to yourself, either. The beginning of mastery is vision; see the miracles around you and that will make it easier for greater miracles to grow.

3. **See yourself in the light.** The ego keeps its grip by making us feel needy and powerless. From this sense of lack grows the enormous hunger to acquire everything in sight. Money, power, sex, and pleasure are supposed to fill up the lack, but they never do. You can escape this whole package of illusion if you see yourself not in a shadow fighting to get to God but as in the light from the first moment. The only difference between you and a saint is that your light is small and a saint's is great. This difference pales in comparison to the similarity: you are both of the light. The irony of near-death experiences is that when people come back to report how rapturously they felt bathed in a blinding light, they overlook that the light was there all along. It is the self.

4. See everyone else in the light. The cheapest way to feel good about yourself is by feeling superior to others. From this dark seed grows every manner of judgment. Getting out of judgment is vital, and to plant that seed, you have to stop dividing others into categories of good and bad. Everyone lives in the same light. A simple formula may help here. When you are tempted to judge another person, no matter how obviously they deserve it, remind yourself that everyone is doing the best he can from his own level of consciousness.

5. Reinforce your intentions every day. On the surface, the obstacles against spirit are enormous. Everyday life is a kind of swirling chaos, and the ego is entrenched in its demands. You cannot rely on one good intention to carry you through. It takes discipline to remind yourself, day in and day out, of your own spiritual purpose. For some people it helps to write down their intentions; for others periods of regular meditation and prayer are useful. It isn't good enough to repeat your intentions to yourself on the run. Find your center, look closely at yourself, and do not let go of your intention until it feels centered inside yourself.

6. **Learn to forgive yourself.** The ego has a way of co-opting spirit and pretending that everything is going well. Thus we all fall into traps of selfishness and delusion when least expected. The chance remark that wounds someone else, the careless lie, the irresistible urge to cheat are universal. Forgive yourself for being where you are. To be honestly a creature of stage two, driven by ambition and haunted by guilt, is more spiritual than pretending to be a saint. Apply to yourself the same dictum as to others: You are doing the best you can from your own level of consciousness. (I like to remember one master's definition of the perfect disciple: "One who is always stumbling but never falls.")

7. **Learn to let go.** The paradox of being spiritual is that you are always wrong and always right at the same time. You are right to try to know God in every way you can, but you are wrong to think that things won't change tomorrow. Life is change; you must be prepared to let go of today's beliefs, thoughts, and actions no matter how spiritual they make you feel. Every stage of inner growth is a good life. Each is nurtured by God. Only your second attention will know when it is time to move on, and when you know, don't hesitate to let go of the past.

8. Revere what is holy. Our society teaches us to be skeptical of the sacred. The usual attitude toward miracles is a bemused caution; few people spend much time delving into the world's great wealth of scriptures. But every saint is your future, and every master is reaching over his shoulder to look at you, waiting for you to join him. The human representatives of God constitute an infinite treasure. Dipping into this treasure will help to open your heart. At just the moment when your soul wants to blossom, the words of a saint or sage may be the right fertilizer.

9. Allow God to take over. When all is said and done, either spirit has power or it doesn't. If there is only one reality, nothing in the material world stands outside God; this means that if you want something, spirit can provide it. Deciding what part you need to do and what part God will do is delicate. It also changes from stage to stage. You have to know yourself in this regard; no one else can tell you what to do. Most people are addicted to worry, control, overmanagement, and lack of faith. On a daily basis, resist the temptation to follow these tendencies. Don't listen to the voice that says you have to be in charge, that things aren't going to work out, that constant vigilance is the only way to get anything done. This voice is right because you listen to it too much. It won't be right if you let spirit try a new way. Be willing to experiment. Your intention is the most powerful tool at your disposal. Intend that everything will work out as it should, then let go and see if clues come your way. Let opportunities and openings come your way. Your deepest intelligence knows much more about what is good for you than you do. See if its voice is speaking to you. Maybe the outcome you are trying to force so hard isn't ultimately as good for you as the outcome that naturally comes your way. If you could give 1 percent of your life over to God every day, you would be the most enlightened person in the world in three months— keep that in mind and surrender something, anything, on a daily basis.

10. Embrace the unknown. You are not who you think you are. Since birth your identity has depended on very limited experience. Over the years you formed likes and dislikes; you learned to accept certain limits. A hoard of objects acquired over time serves to prop up a fragile sense of fulfillment. None of this is the real you. Yet no one can instantly substitute the real for the false. It takes a process of discovery. Because it is painful to strip away so many layers of illusion, you have to let the unwinding of the soul take place according to its own rhythm and timing. Your overall attitude should be that the unknown is awaiting you, an unknown that has nothing to do with the "I" you already know. Some people reach the edge of illusion only at the moment of death, and then with a long look backward, one lifetime seems incredibly short and transient.

Around 1890 a Blackfoot Indian chief was dying. His name was Isapwo Muksika Crowfoot, and he whispered these words into the ear of a missionary father:

> *What is life?*
> *It is the flash of a firefly in the night,*
> *It is the breath of a buffalo in the winter time,*
> *It is the little shadow that runs across the grass*
> *And loses itself in the sunset.*

The part of us that we know already is the part that flickers out all too fast. Far better to seize this time and become timeless. When you feel a new impulse, an uplifting thought, an insight that you have never acted upon before, embrace the unknown. Cherish it as tenderly as a newborn baby. The unknown is the only thing that truly cares about the fate of your soul; therefore it would be good to revere it as much as you revere holiness. God lives in the unknown, and when you can embrace it fully, you will be home free.

ABOUT THE AUTHOR

DEEPAK CHOPRA is the author of more than fifty books translated in over thirty-five languages, including numerous *New York Times* bestsellers in both the fiction and nonfiction categories. Chopra's Wellness Radio airs weekly on Sirius Stars, Channel 102, which focuses on the areas of success, love, sexuality and relationships, well being, and spirituality. He is founder and president of the Alliance for a New Humanity and can be contacted at www.deepakchopra.com. *Time* magazine heralds Deepak Chopra as one of the top 100 heroes and icons of the century, and credits him as "the poet-prophet of alternative medicine." (June 1999).

ENJOY THESE NEW BESTSELLERS
BY DEEPAK CHOPRA

THE BOOK OF SECRETS
Unlocking the Hidden Dimensions of Your Life
978-1-4000-9834-7
$14.95 paper (Canada: $19.95)

PEACE IS THE WAY
Bringing War and Violence to an End
978-0-307-33981-2
$13.00 paper (Canada: $18.00)

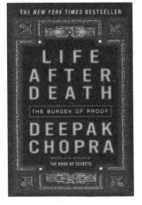

LIFE AFTER DEATH
The Burden of Proof
978-0-307-34578-3
$24.00 hardcover (Canada: $32.00)

Available wherever books are sold.